Real Estate

National Sales Review Crammer

13TH EDITION

HONDROS LEARNING™

4140 Executive Parkway

Westerville, Ohio 43081

www.hondroslearning.com

18 17 16   2 3 4

ISBN: 978-1-59844-269-4

TABLE OF CONTENTS

TABLE OF CONTENTS

"Do it once, do it right, and never do it again!" That is the philosophy I believe in for everything in life—and preparing for your Real Estate Salesperson Licensing Examination is no different. If you've taken all your pre-licensing courses and built a strong foundation of real estate knowledge, the *Real Estate National Sales Review Crammer*™, combined with a Review or Crammer™ Course, and CompuCram® Exam Prep Software are all you need to pass the exam! Here, you'll focus on the concepts, subjects, and topics you need to know for the exam—presented in the format you'll see on the exam!

The quality and effectiveness of Hondros Learning's educational materials are directly related to the knowledgeable and experienced instructors who have contributed to them. Instructional methods and materials can make a major difference in your exam success—but the ultimate responsibility is yours. You have a significant role in making the *Real Estate National Sales Review Crammer*™ work for you, to create the *best opportunity for your exam success*. And, students who also use Hondros Learning's CompuCram® Exam Prep Software consistently increase their opportunities of *passing their exams the first time*!

Successful completion of this course is essential to your career. So, simply put, thoroughly review the information presented here, from start to finish, and you'll not only pass the exam but also be on your way to a rewarding career in the real estate industry! Let's get to it and—do it once, do it right, and never do it again!

—*John G. Hondros*

Test-Taking Techniques

Before you can make application and be seated for your sales examination, you must complete all required pre-licensing courses. Once your application and eligibility for the exam have been verified, you'll be sent a Candidate Information Bulletin from the testing organization. This Bulletin contains most everything you'll need to know about the exam and testing process. It includes information on topics such as:

- Special accommodations for individuals with disabilities
- Testing dates and locations
- Payment of fees
- Scheduling an exam
- Regulations and testing procedures
- Examination structure
- Scoring

It is important that you review the information in this *Bulletin* and refer to it to answer any questions you have.

Since it may have been a while since you've taken an exam, let's start with a review of some basic test-taking techniques. These techniques can easily add 10 to 15 points to your score. Most importantly, though, you need to be relaxed. If you study and prepare, you'll do fine. Telling your family, friends, and colleagues you are taking the exam creates pressure on you by setting expectations. Constant worrying about everyone's expectations for success may have the opposite effect on your ability to comfortably and successfully complete the exam. Go back and tell everyone you have decided to wait a month before taking the exam. Their expectations will disappear, and the sense of pressure will be gone. Try it; it works!

Here are some other pointers:

1. Test moderators enforce the regulations closely. ***NO eating, drinking, or smoking*** is allowed in the examination area and there are no breaks once the examination begins. Calculators must be simple, basic calculators. You are limited to one piece of scrap paper. If you run out of scrap paper, simply hold it up for a replacement. Listen to the guidelines and follow them closely.

2. When you begin the exam, we suggest you immediately write down the concepts and formulas on your scrap paper. This way, you will have them handy when you need them (e.g., capitalization rate formulas).

3. *Read the question. Read the question. Read the question*. Read the question at least **three times** before you look at the answers, and then read the answers at least two times before selecting the best one.

   People tend to read the questions quickly. Don't do this since you'll often read it so fast you will fall into the "sounds alike" trap and confuse words, (e.g., grantor versus grantee, gross income versus net income).

   When reading a question, do not jump to quick conclusions. Before you choose an answer, be sure you have read the entire question and all answer choices.

4. Do not spend a lot of time on one question. Go through the exam and answer only those questions that you ***know*** are correct. If you're in doubt about an answer, skip the question and go to the next one. It's best to move through the questions you can answer as quickly as possible and return to the others later, if you have time. If you are in doubt about a question, "mark" it, skip it, and move on. At the end of the test, after answering the questions you know, go back and review all marked questions, if you have time. Sometimes other questions in the exam will help you answer a question you are unsure of.

5. Maintain your concentration. Sometimes, you may lose your train of thought because a question appears to be poorly written, make no sense, or have more than one correct answer. Getting caught on one of these questions can throw you off for a series of questions to follow. When this happens, relax your mind and your muscles—and skip the question. There may be three or four of these questions on the exam. If, by chance, you miss them because you had to guess, you will not fail. What causes you to fail the exam is becoming so frustrated that you miss the second, third, or fourth question after that. Keep your composure. Remember, even if you miss these and no others, you will still pass.

6. If a question on the exam appears to have more than one correct answer, look for the *best answer* based on the supplied information—not your assumptions.

7. Answer all questions, even if you have to guess. Two of the four answers are often not even worth considering. Narrow your choices by process of elimination—weeding out the obviously incorrect answers, or answers you know are wrong. Pick one of the remaining answers when guessing.

8. Your first answer is usually the right one. Don't change it unless you're sure.

9. Answers with absolutes such as *must*, *always*, *greatest*, *never*, and *has to be* are generally not the correct ones.

10. Be careful of "except" questions. You tend to read these questions too fast and even though you know the correct answer, you will choose the opposite.

> ## Example:
>
> All of the following are examples of a specific lien, ***except***:
>
> a. Property taxes
> b. Judgment
> c. Mechanic's lien
> d. Mortgage
>
> The best way to answer these questions is to cover the word ***except*** or ***not*** when reading the question. (Answer: b)

11. Watch your time to ensure you budget it wisely, but remember time is ***not*** your enemy. You'll have plenty of time to complete the exam as long as you work consistently. Do not spend 15 minutes on one question to get one point, when you could have answered 10 questions for 10 points.

    If you try to answer every question the first time through, you may end up wasting valuable time on the questions you are not sure of. This will only increase your anxiety level. A good time to recognize this pattern is in a Sales Review Crammer™ course— where you're tested using these same types of questions. If you see this happening, make a concerted effort to answer only the questions you know and can complete quickly. After you've regained your sense of balance, go back and answer the difficult questions. If you have used your time well on the review exam, you will be prepared for the real exam.

12. Double-check your math answers by reversing the process, if time permits. Also, national testing companies are fully aware that all calculators round answers differently. This will not be a problem. Many times, the correct answer can be off by as much as $1, $5, or more. Since this is the case, don't let small differences in math worry you. Close counts! Pick the closest answer and move on. Do not waste 10 minutes looking for 10 cents in your answer.

    Caution: Your calculator may not function properly, just when you need it most. Be sure you take two calculators with new and extra batteries.

13. Finally, if you have the time to review the questions you skipped, take time to **read them again completely**. Then, dissect the question into parts (clauses and prepositional phrases). This will help you understand what the question is really asking. This is even true for math questions. When you cannot determine the answer, and before you guess, ask yourself, "What concept is this question trying to make sure I know?"

    Ask yourself which answer best illustrates that concept. Keep in mind that the purpose of The exam is to make sure you have the minimum amount of knowledge needed to function in the real estate industry.

14. Above all—**don't panic!** During the exam, you may lose your train of thought. When this occurs, stop and take a moment to relax. Take a deep breath, let your shoulders drop; relax your muscles and your mind before proceeding. Recall what you have studied. You know more than you think you do—just relax enough to let it become clear.

15. Be positive and have confidence in yourself. Starting today, say to anyone who will listen, "I'm going to pass the exam," and *mean it*!

Remember there's only one sure-fire way to pass the exam—***study.*** This Crammer™ has been developed with that in mind. Follow our directions exactly. To use this manual effectively and pass the exam, read and follow our guidelines. The next section offers tips on studying effectively.

How To Study

Some Basic Points

The Real Estate Salesperson Exam, like other national exams, focuses on concepts, definitions, and calculations. Calculations represent only about 10% of the questions on the exam, but they will be mixed in with the concept questions. There is a very complete math review (Chapters 6 and 7) in this book to help you learn and master math in a non-threatening way. These chapters can help you manage any "math anxiety" you might have. Still, math is a relatively small portion of the exam, so don't fret over it. Instead, focus on definitions.

Our definitions are not just dictionary definitions, but definitions the way you may see them on the exam. Definitions of real estate language and terms represent one of the largest parts of the exam. The definitions are pared down to the most likely words for the exam. Place special emphasis on knowing and understanding all the words in the Glossaries. In fact, the Glossaries are so important, they're not at the back of the book—instead, they're all in Chapter 4, the first chapter you should study!

The concepts in this book are presented in the way you should study them for the exam. Of course, questions will not necessarily appear in this order, but the concepts are organized logically to help you build on your knowledge. The outlines used by the different testing organizations appear in Chapter 3. Again, the outlines are not necessarily in the same order that the questions will appear on your exam, but knowing the topic outline from your testing company will help you study more effectively.

This textbook has been developed using our more than 40 years of proven experience in conducting review courses. If you want to do well on the national real estate sales exam, you should read and understand all concepts covered here. If you can do well on the sample exams, you should be able to pass the national real estate sales exam, as well.

The Basics of Good Study Methods

To create your best chance for success on the national real estate sales exam, it is very important to follow these instructions.

Once you have completed your pre-licensing course(s), immediately begin studying for the national exam by reading this Crammer™ in its entirety and doing the following:

A. Read Chapter 1, Test-Taking Techniques. Put these ideas into practice as you take the sample exams at the end of the book. Learn the techniques so they become second nature. This will increase your exam score by at least 10 points.

B. Be sure to read the appropriate test outline in Chapter 3. The outline does not necessarily represent the order in which you'll see topics on the test, but it will tell you exactly what subjects are covered on the exam and the percentage of questions you can expect in each area.

C. Read *all* of Chapter 4, Glossaries, and *read it no fewer than 3 times!* To help you, it's divided into three sections: General Glossary, Agency Glossary, and Math Glossary. (Some terms appear in more than one glossary.) If a word is in the glossaries, it is in the bank of test questions. A majority of test questions are simply definitions.

   Know the words in the glossaries. When you read the glossaries the first time, *mark the terms you don't know*. Read them a second time, focusing on the marked terms. Highlight terms you still don't know the second time and repeat this review process.

   There's an added benefit to knowing all the terms in our glossaries: **If you do not know what a word means in a test answer, then it is probably NOT the right answer**.

D. As you read all sections of this Crammer™ book the first time, *mark the concepts you don't know*. Read the textbook a second time, focusing only on the marked parts. Highlight concepts you don't know on the second reading and repeat this review process. Focus on agency rules, fiduciary duties, and disclosures. These areas are often missed on the exam. Civil rights laws are also heavily tested. **Read, review, and focus on these areas!**

E. In this book, you will see charts or graphics designed to help in certain areas. These cover things with a good chance of appearing on the exam, in one form or another.

F. Review the basic math formulas in the math review (Chapter 6). Follow the steps in the example that illustrate the formula. Then, do the sample problems to be sure you understand the concept. These formulas have been broken down to the most basic steps. If you can do these, you can do almost all the math on the exam. If there are one or two formulas you can't get, don't worry too much because you should only see these in a few questions on the exam—not enough to cause you to fail.

G. At the end of the book, there are practice exams with questions similar to those you will find on the exam. Grade your exam and review the questions you missed by re-reading those areas in your book.

Golden Rules

If you have studied all the material in this textbook and followed our advice for test-taking techniques and how to study, you should do well on your exam.

Here is a recap of the most pertinent points:

1. *Read the question. Read the question. Read the question!* Read *all* of the answers, too, before you make a choice.

2. Answer all questions, even if you have to guess.

3. Your first answer is usually the right one. So, don't change it unless you're sure.

4. Answers with absolutes such as *must*, *always*, *greatest*, *never*, and *has to be* are generally *not* the correct choices.

5. Know definitions! Study the glossaries in this book—if you don't, you are doing yourself a disservice.

6. If you have thoroughly studied the glossaries and see an answer on the exam containing a word you don't know, it probably is *not* the right answer.

7. For math questions, at least know the circle formula and tax formula.

8. For math questions, when in doubt DIVIDE (÷).

9. If you're not sure of a math question, you can always try plugging in each of the given answers.

10. For math questions, close counts on the exam—don't waste time trying to get an exact match, since rounding may be different.

11. Double-check your math answers by reversing the process, if time permits.

In conclusion, if you do it once, do it right, and do it as outlined in this book, you'll never have to do it again—and you'll be on the road to success in your real estate career!

Real Estate Salesperson Examination:
Outline and Subjects Covered

PSI Exam Overview

The national portion of the PSI salesperson exam covers areas of importance to licensees in order for them to perform their duties to the public in a competent and legally responsible manner. It consists of 80 questions used to compute your score. In addition, a small number (5–10) of "pre-test" questions for future exams may be included. These pretest questions will not be scored and the time taken to answer them will not count against examination time.

I. Property Ownership   (8% – 6 questions)

1. Classes of Property
    a. Real versus Personal Property
    b. Defining Fixtures
2. Land Characteristics and Legal Descriptions
    a. Physical Characteristics of Land
    b. Economic Characteristics of Land
    c. Types of Legal Property Descriptions
    d. Usage of Legal Property Descriptions
3. Encumbrances
    a. Liens (Types and Priority)
    b. Easements and Licenses
    c. Encroachments
4. Types of Ownership
    a. Types of Estates
    b. Forms of Ownership
    c. Leaseholds
    d. Common Interest Properties
    e. Bundle of Rights
5. Physical Descriptions of Property
    a. Land and Building Area
    b. Basic Construction Types and Materials

II. Land Use Controls and Regulations   (6% – 5 questions)

1. Government Rights in Land
    a. Property Taxes and Special Assessments
    b. Eminent Domain, Condemnation, Escheat
    c. Police Power
2. Public Controls Based in Police Power
    a. Zoning and Master Plans
    b. Building Codes
    c. Environmental Impact Reports
    d. Regulation of special land types (floodplain, coastal, etc.)
3. Regulation of Environmental Hazards
    a. Abatement, mitigation and cleanup requirements
    b. Contamination levels and restrictions on sale or development of contaminated property
    c. Types of hazards and potential for agent or seller liability.
4. Private Controls
    a. Deed Conditions or Restrictions
    b. Covenants (CC&Rs)
    c. HOA Regulations

III. Valuation and Market Analysis   (10% – 8 questions)

1. Value
    a. Market Value and Market Price
    b. Characteristics of Value
    c. Principles of Value
    d. Market Cycles and other Factors Affecting Property Value
2. Methods of Estimating Value/Appraisal Process
    a. Market or Sales Comparison Approach
    b. Replacement Cost or Summation Approach
    c. Income Approach
    d. Basic Appraisal Terminology (Replacement versus Reproduction Cost, Reconciliation, Depreciation, Kinds of Obsolescence)
3. Competitive/Comparative Market Analysis (CMA)
    a. Selecting and Adjusting Comparables
    b. Factors to Consider in a CMA
    c. Contrast CMA, Broker Opinion of Value (BOV), Appraisal
    d. Price/Square Foot
    e. Gross Rent and Gross Income Multipliers
4. When Appraisal by Certified Appraiser is Required

IV. Financing   (9% – 7 questions)

1. General Concepts
    a. LTV Ratios, Points, Origination Fees, Discounts, Broker Commissions
    b. Mortgage Insurance (PMI)
    c. Lender Requirements, Equity, Qualifying Buyers, Loan Application Procedures
2. Types of Loans
    a. Term or Straight Loans
    b. Amortized and Partially Amortized (Balloon) Loans
    c. Adjustable Rate Loans (ARMS)
    d. Conventional versus Insured
    e. Reverse mortgages; equity loans; subprime and other nonconforming loans
3. Sources of Loan Money
    a. Seller/Owner Financing
    b. Primary Market
    c. Secondary Market
    d. Down Payment Assistance Programs
4. Government Programs
    a. FHA
    b. VA
5. Mortgages/Deeds of Trust
    a. Mortgage Clauses (Assumption, Due-On-Sale, Alienation, Acceleration, Prepayment, Release)
    b. Lien Theory versus Title Theory
    c. Mortgage/Deed of Trust and Note as Separate Documents
6. Financing/Credit Laws

    a. Truth in Lending, RESPA, Equal Credit Opportunity

    b. Mortgage Loan Disclosure and Seller Financing Disclosure

7. Mortgage Fraud, Predatory Lending Practices (Risks to Clients)

    a. Usury and Predatory Lending Laws

    b. Appropriate Cautions to Clients Seeking Financing

V.   Laws of Agency   (12% – 10 questions)

1. Laws, Definitions, and Nature of Agency Relationships

    a. Types of Agents/Agencies (Special, General, Designated, Subagent, etc.)

    b. Possible Agency Relationships in a Single Transaction

    c. Fiduciary Responsibilities

2. Creation and Disclosure of Agency and Agency Agreements (General; Regulatory Details in State Portions)

    a. Creation of Agency and Agency Agreements

    b. Express and Implied

    c. Disclosure of Representation

    d. Disclosure of Acting as Principal or other Conflict of Interest

3. Responsibilities of Agent to Seller, Buyer, Landlord or Tenant as Principal

    a. Traditional Common Law Agency Duties ("COALD")

    b. Duties to Client/Principal (Buyer, Seller, Tenant or Landlord)

    c. Effect of Dual Agency on Agent's Duties

4. Responsibilities of Agent to Customers and Third Parties

5. Termination of Agency

    a. Expiration

    b. Completion/Performance

    c. Termination by Operation of Law

    d. Destruction of Property/Death of Principal

    e. Termination by Acts of Parties

VI.   Mandated Disclosures   (9% – 7 questions)

1. Property Condition Disclosure Forms

    a. Agent's Role in Preparation

    b. When Seller's Disclosure Misrepresents Property Condition

2. Warranties

    a. Types of available warranties

    b. Coverages provided

3. Need for Inspection and Obtaining/Verifying Information

    a. Agent Responsibility to Verify Statements included in Marketing Information

    b. Agent Responsibility to Inquire about "Red Flag" Issues

    c. Responding to Non-Client Inquiries

4. Material Facts Related to Property Condition or Location

    a. Land/Soil Conditions

    b. Accuracy of Representation of Lot or Improvement Size, Encroachments or

       Easements affecting Use

    c. Pest Infestation, Toxic Mold and other Interior Environmental Hazards

    d. Structural Issues, including Roof, Gutters, Downspouts, Doors, Windows, Foundation

    e. Condition of Electrical and Plumbing Systems, and of Equipment or Appliances that are Fixtures

    f. Location with in Natural Hazard or Specially Regulated Area, Potentially Uninsurable Property)

    g. Known Alterations or Additions

5. Material Facts Related to Public Controls, Statutes or Public Utilities

    a. Local Zoning and Planning Information

    b. Boundaries of School/Utility/Taxation Districts, Flight Paths

    c. Local Taxes and Special Assessments, other Liens

    d. External Environmental Hazards (lead, radon, asbestos, formaldehyde foam insulation, high-voltage power lines, waste disposal sites, underground storage tanks, soil or groundwater contamination, hazardous waste)

    e. Stigmatized/Psychologically Impacted Property, Megan's Law Issues

VII. Contracts   (12% – 10 questions)

1. General Knowledge of Contract Law

    a. Requirements for Validity

    b. Types of Invalid Contracts

    c. When Contract is Considered Performed/Discharged

    d. Assignment and Novation

    e. Breach of Contract and Remedies for Breach

    f. Contract Clauses (Acceleration, etc.)

2. Listing Agreements

    a. General Requirements for Valid Listing

    b. Exclusive Listings

    c. Non-Exclusive Listings

3. Management Agreements [Broker Only]

4. Buyer Broker Agreements/Tenant Representation Agreements

5. Offers/Purchase Agreements

    a. General Requirements

    b. When Offer becomes Binding (Notification)

    c. Contingencies

    d. Time is of the Essence

6. Counteroffers/Multiple Counteroffers

    a. Counteroffer Cancels Original Offer

    b. Priority of Multiple Counteroffers

7. Lease and Lease-Purchase Agreements

8. Options and Right of First Refusal

9. Rescission and Cancellation Agreements

VIII. Transfer of Title   (5% – 4 questions)

1. Title Insurance
   a. What is Insured Against
   b. Title Searches/Title Abstracts/Chain of Title
   c. Cloud on Title/Suit to Quiet Title
2. Conveyances After Death
   a. Types of Wills
   b. Testate vs. Intestate Succession
3. Deeds
   a. Purpose of Deed, when Title Passes
   b. Types of Deeds (General Warranty, Special Warranty, Quitclaim) and when Used
   c. Essential Elements of Deeds
   d. Importance of Recording
4. Escrow or Closing
   a. Responsibilities of Escrow Agent
   b. Prorated Items
   c. Closing Statements/HUD-1
   d. Estimating Closing Costs
5. Foreclosure, Short Sales
6. Tax Aspects of Transferring Title to Real Property
7. Special Processes [Broker Only]

IX. Practice of Real Estate
   ## (15% – 12 questions)

1. Trust Accounts (General; Regulatory Details in State Portions)
   a. Purpose and Definition of Trust Accounts
   b. Responsibility for Trust Monies
   c. Commingling/Conversion
   d. Monies held in Trust Accounts
2. Fair Housing Laws
   a. Protected Classes
   b. Covered Transactions
   c. Specific Laws and their Effects
   d. Exceptions
   e. Compliance
   f. Types of Violations and Enforcement
   g. Fair Housing Issues in Advertising
3. Advertising
   a. Incorrect "Factual" Statements versus "Puffing"
   b. Uninformed Misrepresentation versus Deliberate Misrepresentation (Fraud)
   c. Truth in Advertising
4. Agent Supervision
   a. Liability/Responsibility for Acts of Associated Agents

    b. Responsibility to Train and Supervise

    c. Independent Contractors

    d. Employees

5. Commissions and Fees

    a. Procuring Cause/Protection Clauses

    b. Referrals and Finder Fees

6. General Ethics

    a. Practicing within Area of Competence

    b. Avoiding Unauthorized Practice of Law

7. Issues in Use of Technology (electronic signatures, document delivery, internet advertising)

8. Antitrust Laws

    a. Antitrust Laws and Purpose

    b. Antitrust Violations in Real Estate

X. Real Estate Calculations   (9% –7 questions)

1. General Math Concepts

    a. Addition, Subtraction, Multiplication, and Division

    b. Percentages/Decimals/ Fractions

    c. Areas, including Acreage

2. Property Tax Calculations (not Prorations)

3. Lending Calculations

    a. Loan-to-Value Ratios

    b. Discount Points

    c. Equity

    d. Qualifying Buyers

4. Calculations for Transactions

    a. Prorations (Utilities, Rent, Property Taxes, Insurance, etc.)

    b. Commissions and Commission Splits

    c. Seller's Proceeds of Sale

    d. Total Money Needed by Buyer at Closing

    e. Transfer Tax/Conveyance Tax/Revenue Stamps

5. Calculations for Valuation

    a. Comparative Market Analyses (CMA)

    b. Net Operating Income

    c. Depreciation

    d. Capitalization Rate

    e. Gross Rent and Gross Income Multipliers (GIM, GRM)

6. Mortgage Calculations

    a. Down Payment/Amount to be Financed

    b. Amortization

    c. Interest Rates

    d. Interest Amounts

    e. Monthly Installment Payments

XI. **Specialty Areas** (5% –4 questions)

1. Property Management and Landlord/Tenant
2. Common Interest Ownership Properties
3. Subdivisions
4. Commercial, Industrial, and Income Property

Glossaries

General Glossary

ABATE Reduce, decrease. Usually refers to decrease in assessed value of *ad valorem* tax.

ABSTRACT OF TITLE A summary in chronological order of the essential provision of every recorded document pertaining to a particular parcel of land, e.g., liens, encumbrances, chain of title, transfers. An abstract of title does not disclose encroachments, forgeries, and the like and does not, therefore, guarantee clear title.

ACCELERATED DEPRECIATION A general term including any method of depreciation that is greater than straight-line depreciation.

ACCELERATION CLAUSE A provision of a promissory note or mortgage where, upon the happening of a certain event, e.g., default in payment, the entire amount of the unpaid loan balance becomes due.

ACCRETION The addition of soil (known as alluvium) to property by the gradual operation of natural causes (common where properties have frontage on oceans or rivers). This added land becomes the property of the owner on whose land it is deposited.

ACKNOWLEDGMENT A written declaration by a person executing an instrument, given before an officer authorized to give an oath (usually a notary public), stating that the execution is of his own volition, e.g., grantor of a deed.

ACRE A measure of land which is 43,560 square feet.

ACTUAL NOTICE Things you know because of your own senses: eyes, ears, etc. You have actually seen someone living on the property. If you are buying the property, you need to find out why the occupants are living there.

ADJUSTABLE RATE MORTGAGE (ARM) A type of financing available for real estate mortgages on property through which the Annual Percentage Rate charged will differ from year to year according to terms specified by the lender and authorized by the Federal Reserve banking system.

AD VALOREM TAX Latin, "according to valuation." A tax to be paid based upon a value set by the authorities, e.g., real property tax.

ADVERSE POSSESSION The open, notorious, hostile, and uninterrupted possession of the property of another under a claim or color of title of 21 years after which time the adverse possessor may obtain title to the property.

AFFIDAVIT OF TITLE A sworn statement that title is good.

AGENCY A relationship between one person (principal) and another (agent) where the agent is given the right to act on behalf of the principal in business dealings. Agency creates a fiduciary duty on the part of the agent to act in good faith and loyalty toward the principal.

AGENCY DISCLOSURE The disclosure of the relationship in which one party (agent) acts for or represents another (principal) under the authority of the latter.

AGENT One who acts, or has the power to act, for another.

ALIENATION An English term referring to transfer of property from one person to another.

ALIENATION CLAUSE A clause used in a mortgage allowing the lender to call for the full payment of the mortgage (foreclosure) because the owner transferred ownership of the property. This is a type of acceleration clause because it accelerates the time when the entire loan amount is due. Very often referred to as a "Due-on-Sale" clause.

AMENITIES Features, both tangible and intangible, that enhance the desirability of real estate. For example, a marble fireplace, desirable location, soaking tub, historicity of the location, preferred floor plan, or anything with sentimental value to the buyer may be considered an amenity.

AMORTIZATION Payment of debt in regular, periodic installments of principal and interest (as opposed to interest-only payments).

AMORTIZED LOAN A loan that is paid back in regular installment amounts of principal and interest over a specified period of time.

ANNUAL NET OPERATING INCOME (NOI) Net income is income from a property after operating expenses have been deducted, but before taxes and debt service are counted.

Net Income = Gross Income – Operating Expenses. This is a capitalization method that derives a value indication by using annual net income.

APPRAISAL A defensible opinion or estimate of value of real property as of a certain date.

APPRECIATION An increase in the value of property due either to a positive improvement in the area or the elimination of negative factors. Commonly, and incorrectly, used to describe an increase in value through inflation.

APPURTENANCE "Runs with the land." Something that belongs to property and passes with it, but need not be attached to it, e.g., outbuildings, easements.

ARBITRATION The method by which disputes between REALTOR® brokers may be resolved. Disputes are heard by the Arbitration Committee of the local Board of REALTORS®, e.g., a commission dispute.

ASSESSED VALUATION The value of real property fixed for purposes of computing taxes. Assessed value **x** tax rate = real estate tax.

ASSESSMENT A valuation placed upon real property as a basis to set the amount of tax to be levied. Also, the levy or rate to be paid to the government for services provided or constructed by it, e.g., curbs, sewers, sidewalks.

ASSIGNMENT Transfer of any property, real or personal, or any rights therein to another. In real estate, it does not release the transferor from the obligations stated in the contract.

ASSUMPTION An obligation and promise to be personally liable for conditions in a contract.

ASSUMPTION OF MORTGAGE An agreement by a buyer to assume the liability under an existing note secured by a mortgage. The lender usually must approve the new debtor (the buyer) in order to release the existing debtor (usually the seller) from liability.

ATTACHMENT The seizing of property by court order usually, to furnish security for a debt or judgment.

ATTORNEY-IN-FACT A person specifically designated in an instrument, e.g., power of attorney, to do something legally for another in his stead. An attorney-in-fact has a fiduciary relationship with his principal. An attorney-in-fact need not be an attorney-at-law.

BALLOON PAYMENT (BALLOON NOTE) A partly amortized note where part of the principal is reduced by the time the final payment is due. Thus, a lump sum payment of the principal is due at the end of the loan. Very often called "A partially amortized mortgage."

BILATERAL (OR RECIPROCAL) CONTRACT Bilateral or reciprocal contracts are those by which the parties expressly enter into mutual engagements, e.g., real estate sales contract. Each party promises to perform some act.

BILL OF SALE An instrument in writing that transfers ownership of tangible personal property, e.g., furniture.

BLANKET MORTGAGE A single mortgage loan where two or more different parcels of property are offered as security for the loan.

BLOCKBUSTING An illegal act whereby owners are encouraged to sell their properties because minorities are moving into their neighborhood. (Also known as "panic selling" or "panic peddling.")

BROKERAGE The bringing together of persons desiring to make transactions in real estate.

BUFFER ZONE A parcel of land that separates two other parcels, e.g., a parcel between a residential and a commercial strip of land.

BUNDLE OF RIGHTS Legal rights conferred to owners of real property, including rights to mortgage, sell, make improvements, enjoyment, lease, and use property.

BUILDING CODES Government regulations specifying minimum construction and building standards to safeguard the health, safety, and welfare of the public. Building codes are a valid exercise of the government's police power and can restrict an owner's use and enjoyment of his property.

CAPITALIZATION A method of determining the present value of income property by discounting the annual net income by a commonly used rate of return.

INCOME ÷ RATE = VALUE (IRV)

CAPITALIZATION RATE The percentage (acceptable to an average buyer) used to determine the value of income property through capitalization.

CASH FLOW In investment property, the actual cash the investor will receive after deduction of operating expenses and debt service (loan payments) from the gross income.

CAVEAT EMPTOR Latin, "let the buyer beware." The buyer must examine the goods or property and buy at his or her own risk.

CERTIFICATE OF NO DEFENSE A legal instrument used by a mortgagee to stop the mortgage on a certain date where the mortgagor agrees that the mortgage balance is correct, after which date the mortgagee has no defense.

CERTIFICATE OF SALE A certificate issued to a buyer at a judicial sale (foreclosure action) that entitles the buyer to a deed upon confirmation of the sale by the court if the land is not redeemed during the redemption period.

CERTIFICATE OF TITLE Also known in some states as an "opinion letter" by a lawyer who has examined an abstract, giving an opinion stating that title is vested in a particular individual.

CHAIN OF TITLE Successive conveyances affecting a particular parcel of land, arranged consecutively, from the government or original source of title down to the present holder.

CHATTELS Personal property that is tangible. Goods or other items of property, moveable or immovable, which are not real property, e.g., showcase firmly attached in a store. With rented property, such as a store, chattels are personal property of the renter and as such are also considered trade fixtures that may be removed when the lease expires. (Personal property remains as chattel unless annexed to the real property in such a way so that the item becomes personal property; e.g., a fence. *Compare* **Trade Fixtures**.)

CHATTEL MORTGAGE A mortgage deed that creates a lien on personal property.

CLOUD ON TITLE A valid encumbrance, e.g., mortgage or judgment, affecting title to realty.

COMMERCIAL BROKER LIEN LAW A broker in a commercial transaction has an automatic lien against a property that's the subject of a contract, for the contracted commission amount, when the contract is fulfilled and the broker files a lien affidavit in the recorder's office in the county where the property is located. (Residential real estate brokers must sue in court to enforce a commission payment.)

COMMINGLING To mix funds held in trust with other funds. For example: A broker mixes deposits with his funds by putting the deposits in his general account.

COMMISSION The broker's professional fee. Usually a percentage of the sales price. The fee is an amount agreed upon between the principal and the broker. It is NOT set by law or organizations such as the Board of REALTORS*.

COMMON AREA The area owned together by all the owners of a condominium project. A condominium owner will own their own particular unit in fee simple and the common area jointly with the other owners. The common area usually has liability insurance paid by the Condominium Owners Association.

COMMUNITY PROPERTY Property accumulated by husband and wife by the efforts of either during their marriage. Community property laws provide that each spouse has an equal interest in the property so acquired. Community property is not recognized in all states.

CONDEMNATION A judicial or administrative procedure to exercise the right of eminent domain to take private property for public use and justly compensate the owner.

CONDOMINIUM The system of ownership in fee simple title to designated areas of air space plus a percentage of ownership of common elements in the property. The air space consists of the area between the walls, floor, and ceiling area.

CONSIDERATION Something of value given to another to compensate them for entering into a contract. Consideration may be money, personal services, or forbearance from performing an act. An example of "good" consideration is love and affection. An example of "valuable" consideration would be money, real estate, etc.

CONSTRUCTION LOAN Interim financing used during construction of a building followed by long-term financing called a "takeout loan." Loan proceeds are made in installment payments as completion of the improvements occurs.

CONSTRUCTIVE NOTICE Notice given by publication in a newspaper, recording or other method. There need not be actual notice by such publication.

CONTRACT An agreement that the law will enforce. The elements of a contract are mutual assent (offer and acceptance), consideration, competent parties, legal subject matter, and sometimes that the contract be in writing if required by the Statute of Frauds.

CONTRACT FOR DEED A real estate installment sales contract commonly referred to as a land contract. *See* Installment Land Contract.

CONVENTIONAL LOAN A loan that is not guaranteed or insured by a government agency.

CONVEYANCE Transfer of title to land. Includes most instruments by which an interest in real estate is created, mortgaged, or assigned.

CONVEYANCE TAX (or TRANSFER TAX or CONVEYANCE FEE) A state tax imposed on the transfer or conveyance of realty or any realty interest by means of a deed, lease, sublease, assignment, contract for deed or similar instrument.

COOPERATIVE The right to occupy property is obtained through a proprietary lease by purchasing stock in a corporation that owns the property. Owner has interest in the entire building.

COST APPROACH A method of appraisal based on replacement cost minus depreciation plus land value.

COUNTEROFFER A new and contrary offer made as a reply to an offer received from another. The counteroffer terminates the original offer. A counteroffer is a "change."

COVENANT OF SEISIN A promise or agreement of possession under a legal right. One of the five warranties in a general warranty deed. (Also **COVENANT OF SEIZIN**.)

COVENANTS The express promises of two or more parties in writing, the breach of which would entitle a person to damages.

COURTESY The fractional interest of a husband in the estate of his wife at the time of her death. This term not used in all states.

DEBT The amount of money owing on a note or a promise to pay.

DEBT SERVICE The amount of money paid in regular intervals to reduce down the balance owed on a debt. The payment normally has to do with an amortized loan. Thus, it covers principal and interest.

DEDICATION The transferring of real property by a private owner to a public agency (usually occurs from a builder to a city for construction of new streets in a subdivision).

DEED A written instrument transferring the *grantor's* ownership of or interest in real property, if any. (e.g., Warranty Deed, Quitclaim Deed)

DEED IN LIEU OF FORECLOSURE When the deed to a property is given by a borrower to the lender to satisfy the debt and avoid foreclosure. (Also called **Voluntary Conveyance**.)

DEED OF RECONVEYANCE An instrument used to transfer title from a trustee to the equitable owner of real estate when title is held as collateral security for a debt, most commonly used upon payment in full of a deed of trust.

DEED RESTRICTIONS Limitations upon the use of property contained in the deed as a means of controlling the quality or character of a subdivision or specific piece of property.

DEED OF TRUST An instrument used in many states in place of a mortgage. Property is transferred to a trustee by the borrower (trustor) in favor of the lender (beneficiary) and reconveyed upon payment in full. (NOT used in all states, but still may appear on the test.)

DEFEASANCE CLAUSE A clause used to defeat or cancel a certain right upon the happening of a specific event (e.g., upon final payment, words of grant in a mortgage are void and the mortgage is thereby cancelled and title is re-vested to mortgagor). A defeasance clause is often used in mortgages in title theory states whereby the mortgagee agrees to deed property to the mortgagor after all terms of the contract have been performed satisfactorily. A defeasance clause also may be used to give a borrower the right to redeem real estate after default on a note, by paying the full amount due, plus fees and court costs.

DEFICIENCY JUDGMENT The mortgage debt that remains due and payable by the borrower after a sheriff's sale of property. The judgment is actually for the full amount of the unpaid mortgage debt, but the foreclosure sale proceeds are deducted from the amount due.

DELIVERY Act of transferring ownership in real property by documents recognized by law. Grantor delivers a deed to the grantee with the intention of giving up all rights to the property.

DEPRECIATION 1. The decrease in value to real property improvements caused by deterioration or obsolescence; 2. A loss in value as an accounting procedure for use as a tax deduction for income tax purposes. Investors use depreciation as a tax shelter.

DIRECT COMPLAINT PROCEDURES Administrative process where civil rights complaints are heard immediately by the Real Estate Commission, instead of using a hearing examiner.

DISCLOSURE STATEMENT The document commonly referred to under the truth and lending laws (Regulation Z) required to be given to a loan applicant to disclose all of the terms of his loan. Note that other documents also may be referred to as "Disclosure Statements," e.g., Agency Disclosure Statement or Lead-Based Paint Disclosure Statement.

DISCOUNT POINTS An added loan fee charged by a lender to make the yield on a lower-than-market interest rate loan competitive with other higher interest conventional loans.

DISCRIMINATION Treating persons differently. *See* the various Civil Rights laws.

DISINTERMEDIATION The movement of money out of savings accounts into higher yield investments such as corporate and government instruments.

DOWER In some states, a *life estate* that is a one-third estate in real property which the spouse is entitled to claim upon the death of the other spouse on land which the late spouse sold during their marriage.

DUAL AGENCY Representing both parties to a transaction.

EARNEST MONEY DEPOSIT Money given by a buyer upon signing a sale contract showing the buyer's intention to carry out the terms of the sales contract. Earnest money is an inducement and a show of good faith, but it is NOT necessary for a valid contract to exist.

EASEMENT Right acquired by one person to use the land of another for a specific purpose.

EASEMENT APPURTENANT The right acquired by the owner of one parcel of land to use the adjacent land of another for a specific purpose. There must be two tracts of land. One tract is called the dominant tenant (the tract that benefits from the easement). The other tract is called the servient tenant (the tract that is burdened by the easement).

EASEMENT BY IMPLICATION An easement created by operation of law (not express grant or reservation) when land is divided, if there is a long-standing, apparent use that is reasonably necessary for enjoyment of dominant tenement. Also called implied easement.

EASEMENT BY NECESSITY An easement given to a landlocked owner by the court system to provide a way of ingress and egress for the landlocked land. **Remember**: Ingress vs. Egress, and also landlocked land example.

EASEMENT BY PRESCRIPTION A means of acquiring title by long-continued use.

EASEMENT IN GROSS An easement created by law for the good of the public, i.e., utility easement. Remember there is no dominant tenement in an easement in gross.

ECONOMIC OBSOLESCENCE A loss of value due to a change in external factors of a piece of real property, e.g., a steel mill is being built next to your home.

EMBLEMENTS Farm Crops. Tenant farmers' crops may be removed if owner sells the land.

EMINENT DOMAIN The power or right of governmental bodies to take private real estate for public use upon payment of an equitable compensation.

ENCROACHMENT The unauthorized intrusion of a fixture or real property improvement onto the property of another, e.g., the roof of a building that extends over the property line into a neighbor's property.

ENCUMBRANCE Any claim, lien, charge or liability that affects or limits the fee simple title to real property, i.e., easement, liens, etc.

EQUITABLE RIGHT OF REDEMPTION See REDEMPTION, EQUITABLE RIGHT OF.

EQUITABLE TITLE Any interest in real property other than legal title, that a court will enforce and protect, e.g., the interest held by a vendee under a land contract, a lease, an easement, etc.

EQUITY The amount of an owner's interest in a parcel of real estate which is the fair market value of the real estate in excess of the mortgaged indebtedness.

ESCALATION CLAUSE Mortgage or lease clause allowing a holder to vary the interest rate.

ESCHEAT Where real property passes to the state when the owner of such property dies without a will and with no heirs.

ESCROW The process by which money or legal documents are deposited with a third, disinterested party for future delivery so that several acts can occur at the same time and so that all parties to a transaction will have their interests protected.

ESTATE FOR YEARS An estate or interest in land for a definite number of years, months, etc., or expiring on a certain date.

ESTOPPEL CERTIFICATE A statement that prevents its issuer from later asserting different facts. An estoppel certificate is required when a mortgage is sold by the mortgagee. Estoppel is the legal action to seek an estoppel certificate.

EVICTION A court action where a tenant loses possession of leased premises by act of a landlord because of a wrongful act by the tenant.

EXCLUSIVE AGENCY LISTING A listing agreement where the broker is given the exclusive right to sell property but reserves to the owner the right to sell the property himself without payment of any commission.

EXCLUSIVE RIGHT-TO-SELL LISTING A listing agreement where the broker is entitled to collect a sales commission regardless of who sells the property including the owner of the property himself.

EXECUTED A contract that has been performed by the parties. In the vernacular, people use "executed" to mean "signed," but this is not the legal definition.

EXECUTOR A person appointed by a person in his will to carry out the terms of the will and to dispose of his property pursuant to the will provisions. Executors are exempt from real estate licensing laws.

EXECUTORY CONTRACT A valid contract which has not been fully performed. Most real estate contracts are good examples.

FHA Federal Housing Administration, an agency of the federal government created in 1934 to improve housing standards, provide a home financing system to **insure** home mortgages and credit, and stabilize the mortgage market.

FHA LOAN Loans **insured** by an agency of the federal government.

FNMA (FANNIE MAE) Federal National Mortgage Association, an association created under Title III of the National Housing Act to buy Title V loans to keep the market sound. Part of the secondary market (along with Freddie Mac and Ginnie Mae) that purchases first mortgages.

FALSE ADVERTISING Pertaining to real estate: inaccurate advertising of the terms of a loan, under Regulation Z (Truth in Lending Federal Statute) the intent of which is to protect residential buyers.

FEDERAL FAIR HOUSING LAW Title VIII of the Civil Rights Act of 1968 that declared a national policy of providing fair housing in the United States. The law makes it illegal to discriminate in the sale or rental of housing based upon race, color, sex, religion, national origin, handicap, or familial status.

FEE SIMPLE ESTATE An estate where the owner has the highest possible estate: absolute control of a parcel of real estate. Also called a fee or fee simple absolute.

FIDUCIARY A relationship of trust and confidence between a principal and an agent. Fiduciary duties owed by an agent acting as a Fiduciary are (**ACCOLD**):

1. Duty of Accountability,
2. Duty of Confidentiality
3. Duty of Care (Reasonable Care and Skill)
4. Duty of Obedience
5. Duty of Loyalty
6. Duty of Disclosure

FINANCING INSTRUMENTS A commonly used term to describe legal documents, such as mortgages and notes, which are used for borrowing money in real estate.

FIXTURES Personal property attached to the land or improvements that cannot be removed without agreement since they attach to and become real property (e.g., mailbox, chandelier).

FORECLOSURE SALE A legal process by which property serving as security for an obligation is sold when a default occurs. The debtor can be the successful bidder and be awarded the title.

FRAUD An intentional perversion of the truth for the purpose of inducing another in reliance upon it to part with something of value belonging to him or to surrender a legal right. The elements of fraud are (a) intentional misstatement of fact; (b) the misstatement of fact must be material; and (c) the defrauded party must have been entitled to rely on the statement.

FREEHOLD An estate in fee or for life. A freeholder is an owner of land.

FUNCTIONAL OBSOLESCENCE A loss of value due to a decrease in the design usefulness of the property. Examples: having to walk through one bedroom to get to another bedroom, an only bath on the first floor with the bedroom on the second.

GENERAL AGENCY A type of principal agent relationship where the agent is empowered to represent the principal in a narrow area of activities. A general agent has the legal right to bind the principal in any contract within the scope of her responsibility, e.g., a Property Manager.

GENERAL LIEN The right of a creditor to claim all of a debtor's property, both real and personal, seized and sold at public auction, e.g., judgments and IRS taxes.

GENERAL PARTNERSHIP A partnership in which each member has an equal right to manage the business and share in the profits, as well as equal responsibility for the partnership's debts. All of the partners are considered general partners.

GENERAL WARRANTY DEED A deed that includes five warranties, two of which are: 1. Grantor (seller) warrants he has the right and title to convey to the new buyer; 2. Grantor warrants that **all** previous owners in the chain of title had the right to convey.

GRANT DEED A document conveying or transferring real property.

GRANTING CLAUSE *See* **WORDS OF CONVEYANCE**.

GRANTEE One to whom a grant is made, generally the buyer.

GRANTOR A person who conveys his or her interest in real property, generally the seller.

GROSS LEASE A lease of property where the lessee pays a fixed rent and the lessor pays taxes, insurance, and other charges incident to ownership.

GROSS MONTHLY RENT MULTIPLIER (GMRM) The result obtained by dividing the value by the Gross Annual Income, or the Sales price divided by Gross Rents.

GROSS RENT MULTIPLIER A method of determining the value of income producing residential properties.

Gross Rent x Multiplier = Sales Price

HABENDUM CLAUSE Clause induced after granting clause in many deeds (begins "to have and to hold"), describing the type of estate granted.

HIGHEST AND BEST USE An expression describing the use of land that, at the time the property is appraised, results in the highest net income attributable to the land. There can be only one highest and best use at one time.

HOMESTEAD A person's land used as their residence that is usually exempt from attachment by creditors to a statutorily preset amount, i.e., in some states, one can exempt up to $5,000 per owner from attachment by unsecured creditors upon foreclosure.

HOMESTEAD EXEMPTION LAW A real estate tax reduction on a homestead owned by a person 65 years of age or older or permanently disabled.

HUD Department of Housing and Urban Development, a cabinet department of the federal government that administers fair housing laws, and administers FHA programs, e.g., RESPA.

IMPLIED AGENCY Some agency relationships can be implied because of the circumstances surrounding a relationship. Implied agencies do not normally occur in real estate transactions.

IMPLIED WARRANTY A guaranty where the law derives it by implication or inference from the nature of the transaction or the relative situation, or circumstances of the parties.

INCHOATE Incomplete, such as an interest in the real property during the spouse's life, as in dower rights.

INDEPENDENT CONTRACTOR A person retained by another to accomplish a particular result by methods completely up to the independent contractor, e.g., real estate salesperson.

INGRESS and EGRESS Entering and exiting; usually refers to a road or other means of access to a piece of property. An easement for ingress and egress is one that gives the dominant tenant access to the dominant tenement.

INTESTATE A person who dies without making a will, thus his estate is passed on by the laws of descent and distribution.

JOINT TENANCY An interest held by two or more persons in property where each person holds an equal share of interest in the undivided whole and shares equal liability for payment. If one joint tenant dies, his interest automatically passes to the surviving joint tenant(s) by the right of survivorship. Acronym for this is **PITT—Possession, Interest, Time,** and **Title**.

JUDGMENT LIEN A recorded claim against another for a wrongful act ordered by a court. Result of a judgment lien can be the forced public sale of realty.

LAND CONTRACT A method of selling real estate by which the purchaser takes possession and pays for property in regular installments, while the seller retains legal title until the property is paid for in full. Also known as an installment contract or contract for deed.

LAW OF DESCENT AND DISTRIBUTION A system whereby title to property passes by operation of law to the heirs of one who dies owning property without a will.

LEASE A written contract between the owner, lessor of property, and a tenant, lessee, where the possession of land and/or building(s) is granted by the owner to the tenant for a specified period of time for a specified amount of rent.

LEASEHOLD ESTATE The interest of a lessee to use and enjoy real estate for a specified period of time and upon certain conditions, e.g., the payment of rent. The four typical leasehold estates are estate for years, periodic tenancy, tenancy at will, and tenancy at sufferance.

LICENSE A permission, either express or implied, that can be revoked at any time and cannot be assigned, e.g., permission to hunt.

LIEN A claim against title that one party has upon the property of another as security for payment of a debt or obligation, e.g., mortgage.

LIEN THEORY STATE A state in which real estate mortgages are regarded as a lien; title remains with the mortgagor absent default; and foreclosure proceedings can be commenced upon default.

LIFE ESTATE An interest in real or personal property, the duration of which is limited by the life of its owner or the life of another designated person.

LIQUID ASSET An asset, either cash, stocks, or bonds, that can be quickly (within a 24–48 hour period) converted to cash.

LIQUIDITY The cash position of an individual or business measured by cash on hand or securities that can quickly be converted to cash.

LIMITED COMMON ELEMENT That portion in a condominium project owned by all the owners but can only be used by one of the owners, i.e., a designated parking space, the manager's apartment, the balcony off of a particular unit.

LIMITED PARTNERSHIP A partnership made up of one or more general partners and one or more limited partners.

LIS PENDENS A notice filed in the public records for the purpose of serving constructive notice that title or some matter involving a particular parcel of real property is in litigation. Any person who acquires property under a notice of *lis pendens* will take it subject to any adverse judgment that may result.

LISTING AGREEMENT A contract whereby a real estate broker has the right to sell someone's property. It must have a definite beginning and ending date on the contract, e.g., June 1, 2005 to October 30, 2005. A copy must be given to the client upon signing.

LOAN ORIGINATION FEE A one-time set up fee charged by the lender.

LOT-AND-BLOCK DESCRIPTION A method of describing real property that identifies a parcel of land by reference to lot and block numbers within a subdivision, as specified on a recorded subdivision plat, must include county and state.

MANDAMUS Latin, "we command." A writ issued by a court ordering someone to do something or refrain from doing something.

MARKET DATA COMPARISON APPROACH TO VALUATION A method of appraising property where factors considered are neighborhood economic standards, cost of comparable properties, and demand.

MARKET PRICE The price that a piece of real estate actually sold for. Commonly used interchangeably with market value, but not truly the same. *Compare* **MARKET VALUE**.

MARKET VALUE The theoretical price that a piece of real estate is most likely to bring in a typical transaction. The highest price a willing buyer would pay and a willing seller would accept, both being fully informed, with the property being exposed for a reasonable period of time. The market value may be different from the market price a property can actually be sold for at a given time. Market value may be different from market price at a given point in time.

MARKETABLE TITLE A title to real estate that is *reasonably* free of defects and encumbrances so there is no *reasonable* doubt as to its validity or reasonable apprehension of danger or litigation with respect to it, and the owners are insured peaceful enjoyment.

MECHANIC'S LIEN A statutory lien to secure priority of payment for the value of work performed and material provided for improvements to land. The lien attaches to the land and its improvements.

METES-AND-BOUNDS Description of land by boundary lines, terminal points, and angles. The description must begin and end at the same point, POB— Point of Beginning.

MILL Equal to one-tenth of a cent. Used in expressing tax rates. For example, ten mills would be the same as $10 per thousand dollars of value. 1 mill = 0.001 = 1/100th of $1.00

MISREPRESENTATION A statement or conduct by a person that represents to another a fact that is not true. A seller, broker, or builder may have a duty to disclose certain defects in property to a buyer or tenant. Failure to disclose is also misrepresentation. The misrepresentation may be deliberate (known to be wrong), negligent (should have known), or innocent (reasonably believed to be true). Depending on the facts and extent of misrepresentation, there may be a suit for damages, rescission of a contract, or punitive action against the broker (loss of license, etc.).

MORTGAGE BANKER An entity that provides its own funds for mortgage financing.

MORTGAGEE The lender who receives and holds a mortgage as security for a debt.

MORTGAGE NOTE The document, promising to pay back money according to specific terms. The note may not be recorded, but the mortgage deed is recorded. The note is the promise to pay; the mortgage deed is the security for that promise.

MORTGAGOR One who gives a mortgage on his property to a lender, or mortgagee, as security for a loan or performance of an obligation; a borrower.

MULTIPLE LISTING A method of marketing real estate whereby other brokers in an organization are permitted to show and sell property listed with another broker.

MULTIPLE LISTING SERVICE (MLS) A service provided by a local board of REALTORS® that puts homes for sale into a listing book where all members can show the property.

MLS PLUS Also known as "alternative MLS."

NET LEASE A lease agreement that requires the lessee (tenant) to pay taxes, insurance, repairs, operating expenses, and other costs of property.

NET LISTING A listing contract where the seller receives a sum he specifies from the full proceeds of the sale. The broker receives the amount remaining as her commission.

NONCONFORMING USES The use of a structure that, while once lawful, no longer complies with zoning limitations.

NOTE An executed document acknowledging debt by the person(s) signing it. In real estate, a mortgage deed is usually executed at the same time as security for the note.

NOVATION Substituting a new obligation for an old one or substituting a new contract for an existing contract, thus relieving the original obligor from any further liabilities.

OBSOLESCENCE A loss of value due to a decrease in the usefulness of property caused by decay, changes in technology, people's behavior patterns and tastes, or environmental changes, e.g., economic (external) obsolescence, functional obsolescence.

OPEN-ENDED MORTGAGE A mortgage that serves the dual purpose of being security for both the original loan and other future loans. Most mortgages are open-ended today.

OPEN HOUSING The prevention or elimination of discrimination in housing based upon race, sex, color, religion, national origin, handicap, or familial status.

OPEN LISTING A listing agreement where one or more brokers are permitted to show a listed property. *Only* the broker who sells the property is entitled to a commission.

OPTION (CONTRACT) An agreement for which payment is made granting the exclusive right to buy or lease property at a given price within a stated period of time and binding the seller to hold an offer open for a stated period of time. A Unilateral Contract.

PAID IN ARREARS Payment made after it is due. Interest is said to be paid in arrears since it is paid the day of payment rather than in advance, as is rent. Property taxes are also usually paid in arrears.

PANIC PEDDLING *See* **BLOCKBUSTING**.

PANIC SELLING *See* **BLOCKBUSTING**.

PAROLE EVIDENCE RULE A rule of law that limits the terms of a contract to those that are written within it. No oral evidence is permitted at time of trial concerning terms not in the written agreement.

PARTIAL PERFORMANCE The Part Performance Doctrine states that if one of the parties substantially performs his part of the agreement, then the other party may not avoid the contract just because it was not in writing.

PATTERN AND PRACTICE SUIT A lawsuit in which unlawful discrimination is sought to be proven by evidence of patterns of racial discrimination and the practices of individuals charged with violations. Suits are investigated by the Justice Department.

PAYEE The person to whom a debt instrument (e.g., check or promissory note) is made payable to; also known as the receiver.

PAYOFF The payment-in-full of an existing loan or other lien.

PAYOR The sender of the payment.

PER CAPITA Latin, "by heads." One who inherits property under a will, or pursuant to law, does so as an individual, as opposed to inheriting a divided share as one of several representatives of one in whose stead they take.

PER STIRPES Latin, "by lineage." A distribution under a will, or pursuant to law, where children share what their deceased parent would have inherited if the parent had lived.

PERCENTAGE LEASE A lease where the tenant's rent is based upon the monthly or yearly gross receipts made on the premises, e.g., retail lease.

PERIODIC TENANCY A leasehold interest that continues from period to period, e.g., month to month, year to year.

PERSONAL PROPERTY Property that is not real property, but is tangible and moveable; personal chattels, e.g., clothes, furniture, portable dishwashers, microwave ovens, light bulbs.

PLAT (PLAT MAP) A map recorded at the county recorder's office showing how a parcel of land is divided into lots. A map used to show a new subdivision.

POINT A term for a percentage of the loan amount that the lender charges as a fee for making the loan, lowering the interest rate, or other reason. One point is equal to one percent of the principal loan amount.

POLICE POWER Right of the government to pass legislation protecting the safety and welfare of the public.

POWER OF ATTORNEY A legal instrument giving a person the authority to act for another, as attorney-in-fact, not necessarily an attorney-at-law.

PRESCRIPTION EASEMENT An easement created by statute or court action because someone used another's property openly and continuously over a period of time. Thus, even though not a written easement, one was created. Do not confuse with adverse possession.

PRICE FIXING Two or more brokers agreeing to set commission rates. This is illegal and is in violation of the **Sherman Antitrust Act**.

PRINCIPAL 1. The person who gives authority to an agent or attorney, thereby creating a fiduciary relationship; 2. The amount of a debt, excluding interest due.

PROCURING CAUSE The effort that brings about the desired result. An unbroken chain of events that results in the sale of property. Under an open listing, the broker who is the procuring cause of the sale receives the commission.

PRORATION The division of ongoing expenses and income items between the buyer and seller proportionately to the time of use, or the date of closing. *ie.taxes*

PUFFING Exaggerated or superlative comments or opinions, e.g., "This is the most beautiful home in the neighborhood!"

PURCHASE MONEY MORTGAGE A mortgage given by the buyer to the seller as a portion of, or the entire purchase price, of the property. Here the seller is acting as the lender.

QUITCLAIM DEED A deed that grants any interest in property which the grantor may have. The grantee takes the property "as is" because the deed contains the operative words "release, remiss, or forever quit" and does not warrant title or possession. "I will quit claiming all interest in the property, if I have any." Used to release dower or clear clouds on title.

QUIET TITLE ACTION Action by a court to remove a cloud or claim that has been placed on title to property.

RACIAL STEERING *See* **STEERING**.

REAL ESTATE Land and anything permanently affixed to the land. Synonymous with "real property."

REAL ESTATE RECOVERY SPECIAL ACCOUNT Established in lieu of a security bond covering each licensee. In Ohio, the maximum amount an injured claimant may recover is $40,000 per licensee involved in a transaction.

REAL PROPERTY The land and anything permanently attached, such as buildings, fences, and fixtures, including wall-to-wall carpeting, dishwasher, sump pump.

REALTOR® A trade name for a member of the National Association of REALTORS® and its state and local affiliates. All brokers and salespersons are not REALTORS® any more than all copiers are Xerox®.

RECAPTURE The return of monies invested in property, through reduction of the loan amount and/or appreciation. Recapture rate is equal to the rate of depreciation that is allowed for one year.

RECORDING Filing or entering a legal instrument into the county recorder's office, which causes it to become a public record giving constructive notice of its existence to the world.

RECTANGULAR SURVEY Federal government system of accurate land survey and description using base

36 slots

lines and principal meridians. There are **36 Sections** in a township.

REDEMPTION, RIGHT OF The right of a landowner to reclaim property after foreclosure.

REDEMPTION, EQUITABLE RIGHT OF A right of a borrower who has defaulted on a mortgage note to redeem his title by paying entire debt *before* the foreclosure sale.

REDEMPTION CERTIFICATE A certificate used to reclaim a piece of real estate by paying off the debt owed on the property along with any court fees. This procedure is done after a foreclosure sale has been conducted and during the redemption period.

REDEMPTION, STATUTORY RIGHT OF A right of a borrower who has defaulted on a mortgage note to redeem his title by paying entire debt *after* the foreclosure sale. Statutory period can be as long as 1 year. **Not used in all states.**

REITs (REAL ESTATE INVESTMENT TRUSTS) Joint ventures, usually in the form of a limited partnership, through which real estate is purchased. A person must have a securities license to sell REITS. REITs avoid double taxation as they are taxed to the beneficiary.

RESPA (REAL ESTATE SETTLEMENT PROCEDURES ACT) A federal statute requiring disclosure of certain costs and prohibits certain acts in the sale of residential (one- to four-family) improved property which is to be financed by a federally insured lender.

REDLINING The illegal process of a lender denying loans in certain areas of a community because of race, color, creed, etc. An analogous situation exists whenever insurance companies refuse to sell insurance to someone for reasons based on race. **Any decision made that is not based on buyers' qualifications.**

REGULATION Z The implementing provision of the Consumer Sales Practices Act enacted in 1969, which requires disclosure of the cost of credit and various terms available for credit to borrowers and consumers seeking credit. This is a Federal Statute, regulated by HUD, which is not part of any other sections of HUD. Requires disclosure of interest rates as an annual percentage rate (APR) for all consumer loans.

RELEASE The discharge or relinquishment of a right, claim, or privilege.

RELEASE OF MORTGAGE A document signed (and usually recorded) by the lending institution when a mortgage has been satisfied in full.

REMAINDER An interest in land whereby a person receives an interest in real estate upon the death of another, e.g., dad conveys a life estate to son "A," and states that upon the son's death, the estate will go to daughter "B." Daughter "B" has received a remainder.

REMAINDERMAN The one entitled to the remainder.

RESCISSION The annulment of a contract so that the parties to it are put in a position as though the contract never existed, i.e., earnest money is returned to buyer.

REVERSIONARY INTEREST The interest in a life estate that reverts to a *grantor or grantor's heirs* if no remainderman is named.

RIGHT OF SURVIVORSHIP The characteristic of a joint tenancy by which the surviving joint tenant (owner) automatically takes all rights, title, and interest of the deceased joint tenant.

SALE AND LEASEBACK A method for a seller to free capital for his business expansion by selling his property to a buyer who has agreed to lease it back to him.

SECTION A measure of land equal to one square mile, 640 acres, 1/36th of a township.

SECURITIES and EXCHANGE COMMISSION The federal agency that regulates the sale of interstate real estate securities.

SEQUESTRATION The taking of custody of one's personal or real property to compel compliance with a court order.

SETBACK A term used in local zoning ordinances that represents the distance between lot lines and improvements.

SETTLEMENT AGENT The individual, normally working for the title company, who closes real estate loans. The settlement agent is required by FHA guidelines to sign the closing documents along with the seller and the buyer.

SEVERALTY Property held by one person or entity (corporation). Also called sole ownership.

SHERMAN ANTITRUST ACT Name of the federal antitrust law that makes it illegal for brokers to set uniform commission rates (price fixing), and prohibits other acts of collusion.

SITUS Place where something exists; the *personal preference* of persons for one area over another, not necessarily based on *objective* facts of knowledge. Refers to the economic attributes (value, area of preference, etc.) that location gives to a particular parcel of land.

SPECIAL AGENCY A special agency authorizes the agent to represent the principal in a specific activity or transaction, e.g., a real estate broker acting as an agent for a seller.

SPECIAL WARRANTY DEED A deed by which the grantor covenants or guarantees the title from the time he received it until it is conveyed to the grantee. The operative words of such a deed are "by, through, or under the grantor, but not otherwise."

This deed does not have all of the five warranties of a general warranty deed.

SPECIFIC LIEN A lien affecting or attaching only to a certain specific parcel of land or piece of property, e.g., mortgage, mechanic's, and *ad valorem* taxes.

SPECIFIC PERFORMANCE A legal action available to a buyer to compel the performance of the terms of an agreement, such as the sale of a home.

STATUTE OF FRAUDS A law requiring that certain instruments be in writing to be enforceable, e.g., deed, lease, option, but not a listing agreement. A listing agreement must be in writing according to another statute.

STATUTORY REDEMPTION *See* **REDEMPTION**.

STEERING The illegal practice of trying to influence a buyer's choice of housing by racial, religious, ethnic, national origin, ancestry factors, etc. This includes showing only certain neighborhoods, "slanting" property descriptions, and downgrading non-integrated neighborhoods in an effort to influence minority buyers. This may also include a sales associate steering prospective clients to a broker or sales associate of their race, color, or national origin.

STRAIGHT LINE AMORTIZED LOAN A loan where each payment is different, consisting of a fixed amount plus interest on the remaining balance.

STRAIGHT-LINE DEPRECIATION A method of replacing the capital investment of income property, by reducing the value of the property by a set amount annually from the income, over the economic life of the property.

SUBAGENT An agent of an agent; a person that an agent has delegated authority to, so that the subagent can assist in carrying out the principal's order.

SUBORDINATION AGREEMENT A written agreement between holders of liens on a property that changes the priority of mortgages, judgments, and other liens.

SUBROGATION The substitution of one creditor for another, with the substituted person succeeding to the legal rights and claims of the original claimant.

SUCCESSION The transfer of real property by will or the law of descent and distribution, as compared to transfer by a grant of the deed or any other form of purchase or transfer.

SURVEY The procedure that determines the shape, area, and position of a parcel of land by locating its boundaries, and by which a buyer may be sure a property has no encroachment.

TAXATION One of the four powers of the government, used as a means to collect revenue and implement policies. The power of government to tax, among other things, real property.

TENANCY BY THE ENTIRETY Joint tenancy with right of survivorship between a husband and wife.

TENANCY AT SUFFERANCE The interest in real property held by a tenant or mortgagor who remains in possession of leased premises after his right of possession has expired and the landlord has declared he does not want the tenant to remain.

TENANCY AT WILL The interest in real property held by a tenant or mortgagor in possession with the permission of the owner for a term that is not specified.

TENANTS IN COMMON The interest held by two or more persons in property who hold an undivided interest and whose interests need not be equal. There's no right of survivorship between tenants in common.

TERM LOAN A loan whereby interest only is paid in each installment and, at the end of the loan period, the principal is due in full.

TESTATOR One who makes a will; one who dies leaving a will.

TIME IS OF THE ESSENCE Legal phrase meaning that the amount of time stated in a con-tract must be strictly adhered to in order not to breach the contract. The parties specifically contemplate a punctual performance and precise time for completion of the contract.

TIMESHARE An undivided interest in real estate for a period of time. A relatively new type of ownership of real estate used in resort areas. Purchasers buy the use of a property for a certain period of time in each year. Expenses are shared equally among the owners.

TITLE Evidence of legal ownership in real estate. Title is a concept, *not* a document.

TITLE INSURANCE A contract whereby a title insurance company indemnifies the owner that title is free of defects and hidden risks such as forgeries. This does not guarantee you will not lose ownership, only that you would be compensated under terms of the policy.

TORRENS SYSTEM A legal system of land registration, using signature cards, to verify land ownership and determine title status, instead of being recorded (not used in all states).

TRADE FIXTURE Items of personal property annexed to leased property, which are necessary to the carrying on of a trade or business and which are removable by the tenant prior to expiration of the lease, e.g., pizza ovens, bowling lanes.

TRUST ACCOUNT A non-interest bearing bank account, separate from a real estate broker's personal and business accounts, used to segregate trust funds from the broker's own funds.

TRUST DEED An instrument that conveys title to a trustee who holds it.

TRUSTEE'S DEED A deed executed by a trustee conveying land held in a trust to anyone other than the trustor.

TRUTH-IN-LENDING Federal law requires disclosure of the terms of credit by a creditor to a prospective debtor. Regulation Z implements Truth-In-Lending.

UNILATERAL CONTRACT A contract (e.g., Open listing, Option) under which one party makes an express promise or undertakes performance without receiving in return any ex-press promise or performance from other party. No contract occurs until someone performs.

USEFUL LIFE 1. In appraisal for sale purposes, the true economic value of a building in terms of years of use to the owner; 2. For tax purposes, the life set for depreciation. At any time during that period, a new life could begin for a new owner.

USURY Charging an illegal rate or amount of interest on a loan. In Ohio, the maximum allowable rate is 8% above the Federal Reserve discount rate. Ohio usury law does not regulate all government-affected mortgage corporations. Non-exempted loans have a ceiling of 3% above the Federal Reserve discount rate.

VA LOAN A mortgage loan secured through an approved lending institution and **guaranteed** by the Veteran's Administration.

VALID CONTRACT Binding and enforceable contract; one party can legally force the other party to perform.

VARIABLE RATE MORTGAGE Allows lender to increase or decrease the interest rate within parameters set down in mortgage note. *See also* **ADJUSTABLE RATE MORTGAGE**.

VARIANCE A change in part of a zoning requirement without actually changing the zoning.

VENDEE A purchaser in a land contract; the purchaser of real estate.

VENDOR The seller in a land contract; the seller of real estate.

VOID CONTRACT A contract lacking the essential elements necessary for formation; a contract of no legal force and effect, e.g., a contract for an *illegal* purpose.

VOIDABLE CONTRACT A contract that can be terminated even though it appears valid; e.g., a contract with a minor can be rescinded by the minor and thus is a voidable contract.

WARRANTY DEED A deed in which the grantor fully warrants good and clear title to the property and agrees to defend the premises against the lawful claims of third persons. *See also* **GENERAL WARRANTY DEED**.

WASTE Improper use of property, which hurts its value by a possessor who holds less than fee ownership, such as a life tenant, tenant, etc.

WORDS OF CONVEYANCE A deed clause stating a grantor's intent to transfer an interest in real property. Also called a **GRANTING CLAUSE**.

WRAPAROUND LOAN A form of junior mortgage that may be used when it is not feasible to retire the first mortgage, land contract, or lease-purchase agreement. Title to the real estate does not pass until subsequent payments occur.

WRIT OF EXECUTION A court order directing an official to sell property to satisfy a judgment against the owner of the property.

YIELD Rate of return on an investment, generally shown as a percentage. The yearly income divided by the value of the building equals the percentage of return. IRV—income, rate, value.

ZONING The regulation over the use of land within a specific municipality.

Agency Glossary

AGENCY RELATIONSHIP Under the common law, this relationship is defined as:

1. Agency is the fiduciary relation that results from the manifestation of consent by one person to another that the other shall act on his behalf and subject to his control, and consent by the other so to act.
2. The one for whom action is taken is the principal.
3. The one who is to act is the agent.

   In a real estate transaction, the agency relationship is formed between the brokerage firm (including all their licensees) and the principal.

ALTERNATIVE MLS *See* **MLS PLUS**.

BLANKET UNILATERAL OFFER OF SUBAGENCY An automatic offer that is made by a listing agent to all other members of the Multiple Listing Service (MLS) when the agent submits the seller's listing to a traditional MLS; the offer is accepted whenever an agent shows the listed property without rejecting the offer.

BUYER AGENCY The agency relationship that exists between a buyer principal and the buyer's agent.

BUYER AGENCY EXCLUSIVELY The practice of representing only the buyer and never the seller in a transaction.

BUYER'S AGENT A real estate agent who is employed by and represents only the buyer in a real estate transaction, regardless of whether the commission is paid by the buyer or by the seller, or through a commission split with the listing agent.

CLIENT A buyer or seller represented by an agent who is subject to that buyer's or seller's control; also called a principal.

CONTINGENT FEE Any fee that is conditional upon some event occurring, usually a closing.

COOPERATING AGENT *See* **SELLING AGENT**.

CUSTOMER A buyer who is working with an agent who represents the seller; also the seller of unlisted property that is being sold to a buyer represented by a buyer's agent.

DISCLOSED DUAL AGENCY A dual agency relationship where the brokerage firm, by written or oral means, discloses and receives informed consent from both the buyer and the seller to act in a dual agency capacity.

DISCLOSED DUAL AGENT A real estate agent who has received informed consent from both a buyer and seller in the same transaction to act in a dual agency capacity.

DUAL AGENCY An agency relationship where the brokerage firm represents both the buyer and the seller in the same transaction to act in a dual agency capacity.

FACILITATOR A person who assists the parties to a potential real estate transaction in communication, interposition, and negotiation, to reach agreement between or among them, without being an advocate for the interests of any party except the mutual interest of all parties to reach agreement. Also known as an intermediary. (Not recognized in all states.)

FIDUCIARY DUTIES Duties owed by an agent to his principal (**ACCOLD**):

1. **Duty of Accountability** Acknowledges that all money received in the agency relationship belongs to the principal, not the agent. The agent has the duty to strictly account for any amounts received in a transaction on behalf of the principal.
2. **Duty of Confidentiality** An agent has the duty to keep confidential any and all information that may harm the agent's client(s). The only instance in which such information can—and must—be relinquished is in the case of a court order.
3. **Duty of Care (Reasonable Care and Skill)** Must be used by an agent at all times when acting on behalf of a client. Agents are seen as trusted professionals and experts, and as such are held to a minimum standard of competence. Expertise should never be claimed in areas where one does not have special training, and agents must be careful never to engage in the unauthorized practice of law.
4. **Duty of Obedience** Agents must follow all legal directions of the principal, obey the restrictions of the agency relationship, and not stray beyond scope of authority.
5. **Duty of Loyalty** Agents must put the principal's best interests above all others, including the agent's own; and agents must not reveal confidential information.
6. **Duty of Disclosure** An agent is obligated to disclose to his principal all relevant and material information, unless obtained through a previous fiduciary relationship, that the agent knows and that pertains to the scope of the agency. Duties of disclosure include: true property value, all offers to purchase, identity of the prospective buyer, buyer's financial condition, any relationship between the buyer and the broker, and any commission splitting arrangements with other brokers.

IMPLIED AGENCY Any agency relationship that is indicated by the words and/or actions of the agent rather than by written agreement; also called accidental or undisclosed agency.

INFORMED CONSENT A person's agreement to allow something to happen that is based on a full disclosure of facts needed to make the decision intelligently, e.g., knowledge of liability involved, alternatives, etc.

IN-COMPANY SALE A sale in which one real estate brokerage company acts as both the listing and selling agent.

INTERMEDIARY *See* **FACILITATOR**.

LISTING AGENT An agent of the seller who markets that seller's property, usually exclusively, and represents the seller during the sale and closing of the property. Also known as "seller's agent."

MULTIPLE LISTING SERVICE (MLS) An organized system created to disseminate information about listed properties and through which members offer cooperation and compensation to their participants; usually a committee of a Board or a corporation owned by a Board.

MLS PLUS MLS policy that allows listing agents to indicate the fee they will pay a buyer's agent as well as the fee they will pay to a subagent upon a successful closing. An offer of subagency is mandatory. Also known as "alternative MLS," but is *not* in all markets.

PARTICIPATING AGENT *See* **SELLING AGENT**.

PROCURING CAUSE The proximate cause originating a series of events that, without break in their continuity, results in the accomplishment of the objective. A real estate broker will be regarded as the "procuring cause" of a sale, so as to be entitled to commission, if the broker's efforts are the foundation on which the negotiations resulting in a sale are begun.

SELLER'S AGENT A real estate agent who is employed by and represents only the seller in a real estate transaction. Also known as "listing agent."

SELLER AGENCY The agency relationship that exists between a seller principal and the seller's agent.

SELLER AGENCY AND BUYER AGENCY WITH DISCLOSED DUAL AGENCY FOR IN-COMPANY SALES The practice of representing the party you are working with (either buyer or seller) and becoming a disclosed dual agent for in-company sales.

SELLER AGENCY EXCLUSIVELY The practice of representing only the seller and never the buyer in a transaction.

SELLING AGENT Any agent who sells a property; she may be the subagent or listing agent of the seller, or a buyer's agent, or a dual agent. Also called a cooperating agent, or participating agent.

SINGLE AGENCY The practice of representing either the buyer or the seller, but never both, in the same transaction.

SPLIT AGENCY A situation in which one agent represents the buyer and another agent from the same real estate brokerage represents the seller. The broker and all management-level employees are dual agents of both buyer and seller. The broker may also appoint a specific agent to represent the seller and another specific agent (from the same firm) to represent the buyer. Also termed an "in-company transaction."

SUBAGENT An agent employed to act for another agent in performing functions undertaken for a principal, who owes the same duties and responsibilities to the principal as the principal's agent. Correspondingly, the subagent can create the same liabilities for the agent and principal that the agent can create for the principal himself or herself.

SUBAGENCY OPTIONAL MLS MLS in which listing agents must offer cooperation but don't automatically offer subagency; the offer of compensation may be to buyer's agents, subagents and/or listing agents; subagency may be offered.

UNDISCLOSED DUAL AGENCY A dual agency relationship that occurs when a listing agent or subagent acts or speaks as though he also represents the buyer but without either written or oral disclosure. Conversely, dual agency also occurs when an agent of the buyer acts or speaks as if he also represents the seller.

Math Glossary

ACRE A measure of land that is 43,560 square feet.

ACCELERATED DEPRECIATION A general term including any method of depreciation that is greater than straight-line depreciation.

AMORTIZATION Payment of debt in regular, periodic installments of principal and interest (as opposed to interest-only payments).

AMORTIZED LOAN A loan that is paid back in regular installment amounts of principal and interest over a specified period of time.

ANNUAL NET OPERATING INCOME (NOI) The income from a property after operating expenses have been deducted, but before taxes and debt service are counted:

Net Income = Gross Income − Operating Expenses

This is a capitalization method that derives a value indication by using annual net income.

APPRECIATION An increase in the value of property due to either a positive improvement of the area or the elimination of negative factors. Commonly, and incorrectly, used to describe an increase in value through inflation.

ASSUMPTION OF MORTGAGE An agreement by a buyer to assume the liability under an existing note secured by a mortgage. The lender usually must approve the new debtor (the buyer) in order to release the existing debtor (usually the seller) from liability.

ASSESSED VALUATION The value of real property fixed for purposes of computing taxes:

Assessed Value **x** Tax Rate = Real Estate Tax

ASSESSED VALUE Value placed on property for property tax purposes by a tax assessor.

CAPITALIZATION A method of determining the present value of income property by discounting the annual net income by a commonly used rate of return.

*I*ncome ÷ *R*ate = *V*alue (Remember: **IRV**)

CAPITALIZATION RATE The percentage (acceptable to an average buyer) used to determine the value of income property through capitalization.

CASH FLOW In investment property, the actual cash the investor will receive after deducting operating expenses and debt service (loan payments) from the gross income.

CONVENTIONAL LOAN A real estate loan, mortgage, or deed of trust *not* obtained under a government-insured program.

CONVEYANCE Transfer of title to land. Includes most instruments by which an interest in real estate is created, mortgaged, or assigned.

CONVEYANCE TAX(OR TRANSFER TAX OR CONVEYANCE FEE) A tax imposed on the transfer or conveyance of realty or any realty interest by means of a deed, lease, sublease, assignment, contract for deed, or similar instrument. Tax can be at the state or county level.

DEBT SERVICE The amount of money paid in regular intervals to reduce the balance owed on a debt. The payment normally amortizes a loan, thus it typically includes principal and interest.

DEPRECIATION 1. The decrease in value to real property improvements caused by deterioration or obsolescence; 2. A loss in value as an accounting procedure for use as a tax deduction for income tax purposes. Investors use depreciation as a tax shelter.

DISCOUNT POINTS An added loan fee charged by a lender to increase the yield on a lower-than-market interest rate loan, making it competitive with other higher interest loans.

EARNEST MONEY DEPOSIT Money given by a buyer upon signing a sales contract, showing the buyer's intention to carry out the terms of the contract. Earnest money is an inducement and a show of good faith (*not* consideration), and is *not* necessary for a valid contract to exist.

GROSS MONTHLY RENT MULTIPLIER (GMRM) The result obtained by dividing the value of a property by the gross annual income, or the sales price divided by gross rents.

GROSS RENT MULTIPLIER A method of determining the value of income producing residential properties: Gross Rent **x** Multiplier = Sales Price

LOAN ORIGINATION FEE A one-time set up fee charged by the lender.

MARKET PRICE The price that a piece of real estate actually sold for. (Commonly used interchangeably with market value, but not truly the same. *Compare:* **Market Value**.)

MARKET VALUE The theoretical price that a piece of real estate is most likely to bring in a typical transaction. The highest price a willing buyer would pay and a willing seller would accept, both being reasonably informed, with the property being exposed for a reasonable period of time. The market value may be different from the market price a property can actually be sold for at a given time. Market value may be different from market price at a given point in time.

MILL Equal to one-tenth of a cent, used in expressing tax rates. For example, ten mills would be the same as $10 per thousand dollars of value. (1 mill = 0.001 = 1/100th of $1.00)

PAID IN ARREARS Payment made after it is due. Interest is said to be paid in arrears since it is paid the day of payment (after a person has had use of the money) rather than paid in advance (which is how rent is typically paid). Property taxes are also usually paid in arrears.

PAYEE The person to whom a debt instrument (e.g., check or promissory note) is made payable; also known as the receiver. ("Pay to the order of: the payee...")

PAYOFF The payment in full of an existing loan or other lien.

PAYOR The sender of the payment.

POINT A term for a percentage of the loan amount that the lender charges as a fee for making the loan, lowering the interest rate, or other reason. One point is equal to one percent of the *principal* loan amount (*not* the purchase price of a property).

PRINCIPAL 1. The person who gives authority to an agent or attorney, thereby creating a fiduciary relationship; 2. The amount of a debt, excluding interest due.

PRORATION The division of expenses and income items between the buyer and seller, proportionately, based on the time of use, or the date of closing.

RECAPTURE The return of money invested in property, via reduction of the loan amount and/or appreciation. Recapture rate is equal to the rate of depreciation that's allowed for one year.

SECTION A measure of land equal to one square mile, 640 acres, 1/36th of a township.

STRAIGHT LINE AMORTIZED LOAN A loan with each payment being different, consisting of a fixed amount plus interest on the remaining balance.

STRAIGHT-LINE DEPRECIATION A method of replacing the capital investment of income property, by reducing the value of the property by a set amount annually from the income, over the economic life of the property.

TERM LOAN A loan whereby interest only is paid in each installment, with the principal due in full at the end of the loan period.

USEFUL LIFE 1. In appraisal, for sale purposes, the true economic value of a building in terms of years of use to the owner; 2. For tax purposes, the life set for depreciation. At any time during that period, a new life could begin for a new owner.

USURY Charging an illegal rate or amount of interest on a loan. The rate that constitutes usury varies by state.

YIELD Rate of return on an investment, generally shown as a percentage. The yearly income divided by the value of the building equals the percentage of return. (Remember: IRV)

General Real Estate Law And Concepts

I. Essential Elements of a Valid and Enforceable Contract

A. Offer and Acceptance

B. Consideration: Something of value must be exchanged (either money, valuable goods, or a promise).

C. Capacity: All parties to a contract must have legal capacity, competency, to enter into it.

D. Legal subject matter: The contractual subject matter must be legal.

E. Written and signed agreement according to statute of frauds.

√ **Note:** Only A and B are necessary for a valid contract; C, D, and E are necessary for an enforceable contract.

II. Contract Classifications

A. *Unilateral*: Contract contains one promise given in exchange for the doing of a completed act; however, there is no obligation to act, e.g., an option.

B. *Bilateral*: Contract contains two promises; for example, one party agrees to sell, and the other to buy, e.g., a listing agreement.

C. *Expressed*: Parties' intentions are expressed clearly, either orally or in written form.

D. *Executed*: Both parties have fulfilled the obligations in the contract.

E. *Executory*: Something remains to be completed by one or both parties in the future, e.g., land contract.

Agent A broker is an agent of the principal client; salesperson licensees are agents of their broker; salesperson licensees are subagents of the principal client.

Client/Principal A person who has entered into an agency relationship with a licensee and with whom there is a written agency agreement.

Confidential Information All information the client directs to be confidential, which, if disclosed, would have an adverse effect on the client's position.

Customer Any third party with whom a licensee works.

In-Company Transaction Transaction in which the buyer and seller are both represented by the same brokerage.

Management-Level Licensee A licensee who is employed by or affiliated with a brokerage who has supervisory responsibility over other licensees.

Subagency An agency relationship in which a licensee acts for another licensee.

A dual agent must not:

(a) disclose information that is confidential or would have an adverse effect

(b) advocate or negotiate on behalf of either party

(c) suggest or recommend specific terms; **nor act in a biased manner for either party**

Key Terms

F. *Implied*: No words or promises are exchanged, but a contract is implied because of the acts or conduct of the parties. When a contract can be construed to have been created solely by conduct, but not through any form of expression (i.e., neither in writing nor verbally expressed).

III. Legal Effects of a Contract

A. *Valid*: The contract contains all essential elements and is binding and enforceable by both parties.

B. *Void*: The contract has no legal effect because one or more of the essential elements of a contract is missing, i.e., there was no offer, acceptance, consideration. Thus there never was a contract.

C. *Voidable*: The contract may be disaffirmed by the party to the contract who lacks the proper capacity, and only that party. It is, however, binding until disaffirmed. Reasons to disaffirm include:

1. Minors: Contracts with minors are voidable at the option of the minor. Minor may even disaffirm after reaching the age of majority (18 in Ohio), plus a reasonable period of time after that.

2. Duress or undue influence.

3. Fraud: The contract can be disaffirmed only by the victim of fraud or duress.

4. Incompetent party.

D. *Unenforceable*: A party fails to perform, but the other party cannot sue in a court of law for performance. **It is unenforceable by a court of law**. The contract cannot be enforced because statute of limitations has expired or an oral real estate is unenforceable by a court of law.

IV. Performance/Discharge of a Contract/ Breach of Contract

A. Contracts are discharged by:

1. Performance.

2. Substantial performance: Party is not released from liability because of a technical deficiency to complete the terms of a contract.

3. Mutual agreement releasing performance.

4. Impossibility of performance. For example, destruction of the property or the death of one of the parties may constitute impossibility of performance.

B. A contract is breached when it is not discharged or performed; that is, one party has broken its promise to perform. The other party has a remedy.

1. When seller has defaulted, the buyer may:

   a. rescind or terminate the contract

   b. sue for specific performance and force other party to perform

   c. sue for monetary damages, usually an amount that would make the innocent [damaged] party whole

2. When buyer has defaulted, the seller may:

   a. rescind or terminate the contract

   b. sue for monetary damages, usually an amount that would make the innocent [damaged] party whole

   c. declare the contract forfeited and retain the earnest money deposit and other payments already received

   d. Note: Specific performance is not a relief available to the seller.

V. Other Terms to Remember

A. Statute of Limitations: The length of time within which a party may sue; for example, "x" years from date of breach of contract, or "y" years from date of discovery of fraud.

B. Statute of Frauds requires:

1. That certain contracts be in writing before a party can enforce them.

2. All real estate contracts for the sale of land and all leases for more than one year, options for more than six months, must be in writing and signed by all parties.

C. Assignment is a transfer of rights and/or duties under contract.

1. Rights can be assigned, unless the contract expressly forbids assigning them.

2. Obligations can often be assigned, but the original party is *secondarily* liable if the assignee does not perform

3. Differs from a sublease in that a sublease is a new second lease that may include new terms.

D. Novation: substituting a new obligation for an old one, also a transfer of rights and/ or duties under contract.

1. The original contract is canceled.

2. A new contract is renegotiated and redrawn, with the same parties or a new second party.

3. The original party, if replaced, is not liable.

E. Offer, acceptance, and counteroffer: First party makes an offer to enter into a contract; other party can accept the offer exactly as made, reject the offer, or make a counteroffer. Remember:

1. The offer remains open until withdrawn or terminated by its terms.

2. The offer may be withdrawn at any time before it is accepted.

3. Rejection terminates the offer.

4. A counteroffer (a change) automatically rejects and terminates an offer.

5. Once terminated, an offer cannot be reinstated unless it's renegotiated.

6. The offer is terminated by death of the offeror or destruction of an element essential to the agreement.

7. The offer must be accepted in the manner specified (e.g., in writing, by fax) or the offer is not deemed accepted. This avoids "mailbox rule."

8. "Mailbox rule" says that an acceptance not communicated directly, in person or over the phone, is effective as soon as it is sent in the mail, unless contract specified a certain means of delivery for acceptance.

F. Equitable Title: The Vendee's/ Buyer's (in land contract) interest in real estate or the interest a person has after signing the sales contract prior to closing.

1. Often, a person with equitable title will eventually have legal title when all conditions of the sales agreement are fulfilled.

2. Examples:

a. Contract for deed (or land contract) Legal title is conveyed to vendee after contract is paid in full or contract terms are met.

b. Pending sale The period after signing the purchase agreement, but before the transfer of title.

G. Earnest Money Deposit: A deposit made by buyer when entering into a sales contract to show good faith. Earnest money deposit not necessary by law. It's applied to purchase price at closing. If cancellation of contract is due to no fault of buyer, buyer is entitled to return of earnest money deposit.

H. Option: An optionee (e.g., a prospective buyer) agrees to pay money or consideration to optionor (prospective seller) for the right to purchase a property for a certain price within a certain period of time (a unilateral contract).

1. While the agreement is in effect, the seller must sell to the buyer if he chooses to purchase the property.

2. The buyer is not obligated to purchase the property. An option is a contract. It must be in writing.

I. Escrow Agreement: An agreement in which the parties to a contract empower a third party to assist in carrying out the terms and conditions of the contract.

1. Escrow agent must ensure that transaction is closed as sales contract requires, or by additional changes agreed to by both buyer and seller.

2. Seller must deposit with the escrow agent the deed and other documents relating to the title.

3. Purchaser must deposit with the escrow agent the purchase price and executed mortgage and note (if applicable).

4. If the title is unacceptable and the sale is canceled, all parties are restored to their pre-escrow positions.

J. Right of First Refusal: Differs from an option agreement in that the seller must first ask the party with "first rights" if he would like to purchase. If she refuses, the seller may sell to another party. Purchase price has yet to be established.

VI. Types of Contracts Used in Real Estate

A. Agency Agreements: Listing Agreement between seller and broker; and Buyer Broker Contracts between buyer and broker.

B. Real Estate Sales Contract (Purchase Agreement): Between seller and buyer.

C. Option: Between optionor (seller) and optionee (buyer).

D. Installment Contract for deed (land contract): Between seller (vendor) and buyer (vendee).

E. Lease: Between landlord (lessor) and tenant (lessee).

VII. Parties in Real Estate Contracts and Documents

√ **Note:** Remember, always ask yourself: who are the parties to a particular contract the exam is asking about. Knowing the following parties and contracts will help answer over 95% of contract questions on the exam.

The "or"s are doers (or givers)	What is done (or given)	The "ee"s are receivers
A. Grantor (owner)	Deed	Grantee (buyer)
B. Offeror (usually buyer)	Offer	Offeree
C. Optionor (seller)	Option	Optionee (buyer)
D. Lessor (landlord)	Lease	Lessee (tenant)
E. Assignor	Assignment of contract	Assignee
F. Vendor (seller)	Sales contract	Vendee (buyer)
G. Lienor (creditor)	Lien	Lienee (debtor)
H. Mortgagor (borrower)	Mortgage	Mortgagee
I. Trustor (borrower)	Deed of trust	Trustee (3rd party)
J. Condemnor (govt. agency)	Condemnation	Condemnee (owner)

VIII. Regulation Z

Promulgated under the federal Truth-in-Lending (TIL) Act, Regulation Z dictates disclosure requirements in credit transactions. The rules require a general brochure be given to borrowers, certain specific disclosures be made relevant to ARM loans, disclosure of the Annual Percentage Rate (APR), and specific disclosures when advertising consumer credit.

A. Where Regulation Z applies:

1. Loans to individuals

   a. All real estate credit transactions for personal, family, and household purposes are covered, regardless of amount.

   b. Non-real estate credit transactions for personal, family, and household purposes are covered up to $25,000. Loans over $25,000 are not covered.

   c. Real estate purchase agreements are not covered.

2. Business or commercial loans are NOT covered

B. Foremost Regulation Z requirements:

1. Finance charges

   a. All finance charges as well as true interest rate must be disclosed before a transaction is consummated.

   b. Finance charges include interest, service charges, loan fees, points, finder's fees, appraisal fees, investigation of credit fees, credit, and property insurance.

   c. The finance charge must be stated as an annual percentage rate.

2. Liens on residences

   a. Regulation Z requires a "cooling off" period (except on first mortgages) when liens will be placed on principal residence. The customer has the right to rescind the transaction up to midnight of the third business day following the transaction.

   b. The "cooling off period" does not apply to mortgages to finance the purchase or construction of a house.

   c. The "cooling off period" does not apply to purchase agreements.

3. Truth-In-Lending disclosure statement covers all disclosures that the lender must make to borrower. This disclosure statement must include:

   a. Name of the lender/creditor

   b. Amount financed

   c. Notice of right to receive an itemization of all amounts financed

   d. Total financing charge—interest rate plus all fees

   e. Finance charge expressed as an APR

   f. Number, amount, and due dates of the payments

   g. New payment, late payment, and pre-payment provision

   h. Description and identification of the security for the loan

   i. Whether or not the loan may be assumed by another buyer

4. Adjustable Rate Mortgage (ARM) disclosures

   a. The index used to determine the interest rate

   b. Where the borrower may find the index

   c. Explanation of how interest rate and payment are calculated

   d. Suggestion that borrower ask lender about current margin and interest rates

   e. If the initial rate is discounted, a disclosure of that fact and a suggestion that the borrower ask the amount of the discount

f. The rate and payment adjustment periods, and any caps

g. Statement that rate or payment caps may result in negative amortization

h. Statement that the loan has a demand or call provision

i. Description of the information that will appear in the adjustment notices and when such notices will be provided

j. Statement that disclosure forms are available for lender's other ARM loans

k. The maximum interest rate and payment

l. The initial interest rate and payment

m. Conversion option details

5. Restrictions in credit advertising

   a. **Regulation Z does not require lenders to advertise credit terms.** If, however, lenders advertise some credit details (for example, "nothing down," 8% interest, or payments of $550 per month), they must make a complete disclosure of terms.

   b. If advertising discloses *only* the APR, then additional disclosures are **not** required.

   c. The "triggering" terms in real estate ads that then require all disclosures to be made include:

     1. the amount of the down payment (e.g., 10% down)

     2. the amount of any payment (e.g., less than $500/mo.)

     3. the number of payments (e.g., only 180 payments)

     4. the period of repayment (e.g., 15-year financing)

     5. the amount of any finance charge (e.g., 3% to close)

   d. Complete disclosure includes:

     1. cash price or amount of loan

     2. amount of down payment

     3. number, amount, and due dates of payments

     4. finance charge as an annual percentage rate

     5. total of all payments unless the advertisement refers to a first mortgage

     6. amount of real estate taxes and assessments

     7. amount of fire insurance required by lender

IX. RESPA (Real Estate Settlement Procedures Act)

The Real Estate Settlement Procedures Act (RESPA), a federal law dealing with real estate closings, sets forth specific procedures and guidelines for disclosure of settlement costs and regulates other aspects of real estate closing procedures and practices.

A. When RESPA applies:

1. To lenders who invest more than $1 million in residential mortgages

2. Loans where a first mortgage is secured by residential property for the purchase of one to four units (including condos, coops, mobile homes)

3. Second mortgages (by other than seller) and liens for home equity loans

4. Loan assumptions where the loan terms are modified or the lender charges more than $50 for the assumption

B. When RESPA does **not** apply:

1. To sellers who take back a mortgage or note for the entire purchase price

2. Land contracts

3. Loan assumptions where terms are **not** modified and fee is less than $50

4. Loans used to finance the purchase of 25 acres or more

5. Loans for the purchase of vacant land

C. What RESPA requires:

1. Lenders are required to provide a Loan Estimate to a borrower within three (3) business days of a completed loan application.

2. Lenders must provide the Your Home Loan Toolkit by delivering it or placing it in the mail to the applicant not later than three (3) business days after the application is received or prepared.

3. Lenders must provide the borrower with a preliminary Closing Disclosure that clearly shows all charges imposed on borrowers and sellers in connection with the settlement.

4. The Closing Disclosure must be given to borrower at least three (3) business days prior to closing.

5. The Affiliated Business Arrangement Disclosure (AfBa) must be given to the consumer, at or prior to, the time of referral to a second provider, describing the business arrangement that exists between the two providers and give the borrower an estimate of the second provider's charges.

6. Lender must disclose to borrower the possibility and likelihood that the loan will be sold or transferred to another entity or secondary market investor, and the lender's transfer practices, requirements, and procedures.

D. What RESPA restricts:

1. RESPA prohibits kickbacks and fees for services not performed in connection with the closing (excluding real estate commissions and referral fees paid to licensed real estate brokers).

2. RESPA limits the amount of escrow reserves that a lender can hold or require a buyer to deposit into a reserve/escrow account to cover real estate taxes, real estate insurance premiums, or other similar costs.

3. The sale of property may not be conditioned on the use of a particular title insurer or escrow company chosen by the seller.

X. Accounting for Charges (Debits) and Credits to the Buyer and Seller

A. Accrued Items (expenses): Items that have been earned during the occupancy or ownership of the seller, but have not been paid, e.g., taxes

B. Prepaid Items: Items that have been prepaid by the seller, but have not been fully used up, e.g., insurance

C. Proration Procedures:

1. Determine what item is to be prorated, e.g., loan interest, fuel bills

2. Determine whether it is an accrued item

3. Determine whether it is a prepaid item

4. Determine which method of calculating prorations should be used:

a. Statutory Method: Assume a 360-day year, 30-day month. This method is usually used in prorating mortgage interest, general real estate taxes, and insurance premiums

b. Per Annum Method: Assume a 365-day year, calendar number of days per month (real world)

c. Most exams will specify; if not, use regular months

Real Estate Characteristics and Ownership

Real Property versus Personal Property

Property is defined as the right of ownership in a thing, such as the right to use, possess, transfer, or encumber it. There is real property (also called "realty") and personal property (also called "personalty" or "chattels").

1. Real property is:

    A. The land and everything attached to it (attachments)

    B. The rights of ownership in real estate (appurtenances)

2. Personal property is:

    A. All tangible items not permanently attached to the land

    B. Exceptions include items such as keys

3. When land is transferred, the law says that, unless otherwise agreed in advance, all real property is included in the transfer, but personal property that happens to be on the land is not included. *Usually*, if property is moveable and not fixed to the land, it's personal property.

4. When courts look at real versus personal property disputes, there are two main questions:

    1. What was the intention of the annexer? (Annexer is the person who brought something or put something on the land.)

    2. What was the purpose of the annexation? (Annexation is the act of bringing something or putting something on land. Was the item brought onto the land for personal enjoyment or to improve the land?)

    A. Nature of the item and manner of annexation are viewed as objective evidence of intent. For example:

        1. A birdbath merely out on the lawn would likely be considered personal property

        2. A birdbath encased in concrete would likely be considered real property

    B. Physical attachment is considered, but not decisive. For example:

        1. Keys are not physically attached, but are considered real property

        2. An area rug that is loosely tacked down on the corners to keep it from sliding would likely be ruled personal property

    C. Value of item is rarely considered (but see D)

    D. Difficulty and cost of removal is often considered, as well as potential damage caused by any removal

    E. Relationship of parties is considered

        1. Courts favor buyer over seller

        2. Courts favor lender over borrower

        3. Courts favor tenant over landlord

    F. Trade fixtures can be removed by a business tenant

    G. Written agreements between parties are always enforced

Real estate refers to actual physical land, all things attached to it, and the rights of ownership in real estate. (The terms "real property" and "real estate" are often used interchangeably.)

1. Attachments are things that are attached to real estate, and thus become part of the real property. There are two types of attachments:

    A. Natural attachments (e.g., plants or trees)

1. Note: crops are real property while they are in the ground, but become personal property once they are harvested.

2. Note: "doctrine of emblements" says that a tenant farmer may return to pick the first crop after land has been sold.

B. Man-made attachments (e.g., fences or buildings) are called *fixtures*.

1. *Improvements* are major fixtures, such as a building.

2. *Trade fixtures* are items attached by a tenant for use in business, and are an exception to the rule because they may be removed by the tenant when the lease is over.

2. *Appurtenances* are rights that go along with, or relate to, real estate. These include, but are not limited to:

A. Air rights (with limits for air traffic)

B. Water rights (owners of land adjacent to water have rights to use and enjoy the water—but not ownership of the water.

1. *Riparian rights* are rights of landowner adjacent to a river

2. *Littoral rights* are rights of landowner adjacent to a lake

3. *Appropriative rights* are granted by a government permit to use water for irrigation on non-adjacent land or for other special purposes.

C. Mineral rights (like all rights, these may be sold separately from the land).

3. *Bundle of rights* is the right of ownership in real estate. The bundle consists of:

A. Right of use

B. Right of enjoyment

C. Right of disposal

One who secures the entire bundle of rights is said to be the "owner."

I.   Interests in Real Estate

A. All interests in real estate are subject to certain governmental powers: right to regulate laws (police power, eminent domain, zoning, etc.), and revenue generating laws (taxation).

B. Estates in land: the degree, quality, nature, and extent of interest an individual has in real property. There are two types of estates in land:

1. Freehold Estates

   a. Fee simple "absolute" (fee, fee simple) estate: This is the best interest in real estate recognized by law; it represents the most complete ownership. "Fee" literally translated means, "I own the property"; simple refers to "ownership forever" of the property until the owner chooses to divest him/herself of the property.

      1. It includes all rights incident to property (bundle of rights).

      2. It endures forever and is inheritable and transferable.

   b. Determinable fee or conditional fee: Similar to fee simple, this interest, however, is limited by a condition on the estate. Party may hold the estate only as long as some specified act or condition does or does not occur. Key words are "as long as."

      1. For example, in deed, one party grants property to a second party as long as it is used as a church. If the grantee (second party) uses the property for a store, then his interest automatically terminates and reverts back to grantor (first party) without taking any court action.

   2. Determinable fee may end automatically

   3. Conditional fee is the same thing for purposes

   c. Life estate: This differs from fee simple and determinable fee in that the estate cannot be passed on to the life estate holder's heirs. For example, in deed, one party grants property to a second party for life, thereafter to a third party.

   1. Normally, a life estate is granted for the life of the holder of the estate, called an ordinary life estate; if dependent upon the life of another, it is called a life estate "pur autre vie." (French, "for the life of another.")

   2. Rights and duties of the life estate holder during that holder's life:

      a) Life tenant may receive income from property.

      b) Life tenant may sell, lease, or mortgage the life interest.

      c) Life tenant may pay real estate taxes on property.

   3. Limitations of the life tenant's rights: The tenant may not damage (waste) the property nor harm the rights of the grantor or third party, who will later hold the property.

   4. Reversion: At the termination of the life estate, the property reverts to the **grantor or the grantor's heirs**. For example, "A" grants to "B" for life. "A," the grantor, has a reversion; "B," the grantee, has a life estate.

   5. Remainder: At the termination of the life estate, the property passes to a third party. The third party is referred to as a remainderman. For example, "A" grants to "B" for life, then to "C" and his heirs. "A" is the grantor; "B," the grantee, has a life estate; **"C" and his heirs** are the remaindermen.

   6. Types of legal life estates:

      a) Dower may be released by a prenuptial agreement or by quitclaim deed.

      b) Homestead: A tract of land that enjoys protection from certain debts; the land must be occupied as the principal residence. Currently in Ohio this is $5,000 per owner exemption from attachment by creditors.

2. Leasehold Estates

   a. Types of leasehold estates:

   1. Estate for Years: The lease is in effect until a specified expiration date or until the end of a specified term, i.e., end of the month, end of the year, etc. The length of the lease may span from less than one year to many years. No notice of termination is required; when it is over, it is over.

   2. Period to Period (Estate from Year to Year): No specific expiration date is set, although the length of the period (e.g., month to month) is agreed upon by both parties. As long as the lease is not terminated, it automatically renews at the end of each period. Notice of termination equal to the lease period is required to end the lease.

   3. Tenancy at Will: This tenancy occurs with the consent of the landlord and runs for an indefinite period of time; for example, a tenant may be allowed to occupy a building until it is demolished. The death of either party or minimum notice required by law terminates this type of tenancy. Tenancy at will is not recognized in all states.

   4. Tenancy at Sufferance: The tenant continues to occupy a property after his or her rights are terminated, without the consent of the landlord. For example, unauthorized hold over after a lease expires.

   b. Classification of leases by method of rent payment.

1. Gross Lease: The tenant pays fixed amount of rent and landlord pays the expenses (typical residential lease).

2. Net Lease: The tenant pays the expenses (taxes, insurance, and/or maintenance) in addition to a fixed rent (typical commercial lease).

3. Percentage Lease: The tenant pays a percentage of gross sales (not from profit) earned from the property as rent. This arrangement is often used in shopping centers.

4. Ground Lease: A long-term lease of land (e.g., 99 years). During the term of the lease, the tenant usually operates the property as though it were tenant-owned and may construct buildings on it.

5. Variable Lease: Rent changes periodically during the lease term. The amount of change could be specified in the lease or depend on an outside index such as the Consumer Price Index.

II. How Ownership is Held

A. Basic ways to hold ownership:

1. In severalty: By a sole owner

2. Co-ownership: By two or more owners

3. In trust: By a third party, for one or more persons

B. Co-ownership.

1. Tenancy in common: Two or more holders own a fraction of an undivided interest of the whole.

   a. Fractions may differ among owners; for example, one owner may hold two-thirds interest and the other one-third.

   b. Co-owner may pass interest on to heirs or sell it.

   c. Co-owner may sue to partition; either divide interests into separate parts or force a sale to release his interest in property.

   d. If the character of a tenancy is not specified, as in tenancy by entireties or joint tenancy, most states assume tenancy in common.

   e. No rights of survivorship exist among co-tenants.

2. Joint Tenancy: Two or more holders own a fraction of an undivided interest

   a. Fractions are always equal, usually one-half undivided interest.

   b. Right of survivorship applies, so survivors get deceased's share.

   c. Four unities are required: Possession, Interest, Time, and Title.

   Acronym = **(PITT). P = All have the right to possession.**

   I **= All have an equal interest. T = All have acquired an interest at same time. T = ONE deed of conveyance exists.**

   d. It can be created only by will or deed; it **can't** be implied by law.

   e. A joint tenant may sell or convey her interest during her lifetime, but the successor is a tenant in common with the other tenant(s). Only the last surviving tenant can pass property on to heirs by will or descent.

   f. Joint tenants may sue for partition of property.

   g. No dower, courtesy, or inheritance rights exist under this type of ownership.

4. Tenancy by the entirety: This tenancy is only available in some states. Tenants must be husband and wife, each owning a one-half undivided interest. Ownership in Trust is another form of co-ownership because of two different interests being held.

5. Ownership in Trust:

    a. Another form of co-ownership—two different interests being held.

    b. How interests work:

        1. Trustor creates the trust

        2. Trustee is the party who holds the property for the beneficiary (Trustee holds legal title)

        3. Beneficiary is the party who receives the benefit of the Trust (Beneficiary hold equitable title)

6. Other Forms of Co-Ownership:

    a. Condominiums

        1. By definition, an owner of a condominium owns his designated unit of airspace in fee simple absolute.

        2. An individual owns a unit in fee simple and an undivided percentage interest in the common elements as a tenant in common (e.g., sidewalks, pool, tennis courts, etc.).

        3. Taxes, mortgages, and assessments are liens against individual interests only. There is no separate tax statement for common areas.

    b. Cooperatives

        1. Land and building are owned by a corporation.

        2. Purchasers hold stock in the corporation and receive a proprietary lease for an apartment unit.

        3. Mortgage, taxes, liens, and legal responsibility lie with the entire parcel, not the lease's shareholder. This is an important difference from condominiums.

    c. Ownership by a corporation: Stockholders are not liable for the debts of the corporation.

    d. Ownership by general partnership: Partners are liable for the debts of the partnership.

    e. Ownership by limited partnership: Limited partners are not liable for the debts of the partnership; general partners are.

    f. Ownership by Real Estate Investment Trust: REITS are joint ventures usually in the form of a limited partnership where real estate is purchased. Shares are sold to investors. A person must have a securities license to sell REITS.

    g. Real estate syndication: A group of two or more investors or a joint venture formed as a corporation or partnership to own real estate.

III. Types of Deeds

A deed is the document that conveys the grantor's title to real estate, if any; it is not proof of ownership. It must be signed by the grantor or by the attorney-in-fact, pursuant to a power of attorney.

A. Warranty Deed (General Warranty Deed): When the seller "conveys and warrants" good title, she is providing the buyer with the greatest protection that a deed can possibly give. A title insurance policy is still recommended for the buyer.

Basic covenants are:

1. Seisin: The seller has the right to convey ownership.

2. Against encumbrance: The property is free from liens except as noted in the deed.

3. Quiet enjoyment: The buyer can quietly enjoy the property without good claims on it by third parties.

4. Warrant forever: The seller's warranty is good now and forever.

5. Further assurance: The grantor gives assurance with respect to acts of previous owners in the chain of title.

B. Special Warranty Deed (Limited Warranty Deed):

1. Owner warrants only that he has not done anything to harm title.

2. This warranty covers only the period of time when the seller owned the property.

C. Quitclaim Deed: The seller gives no covenants or warranties, not even that she has any interests in the property. The seller is only agreeing to convey whatever interest, if any, he has in the property; often used to cure title defects and divorces to release legal dower rights.

D. Special purpose deeds, e.g., sheriff's deed, trustee's deed, etc.

E. Transfer on Death Deed: New deed recognized in some states that allows an owner to designate on a deed (instead of a will) who is to receive the real estate immediately upon the death of the owner, thus avoiding the Probate process.

IV. Recording Deeds and Passing Title

A. In most cases, title and responsibility for risk transfer when an executed deed is delivered.

B. Exception: Closing in escrow. Although title passes when the deed is delivered, the date of passing falls back to the date the deed was placed in escrow. If escrow does not close, however, no title passes.

C. The deed is recorded for protection against a third party.

1. Recording gives constructive notice to the world of the buyer's interest. It does not make it legal and is not the time when title transfers.

2. When there are conflicting claims to a property, the one that was recorded first usually has priority. Main exceptions are:

a. Actual notice: Persons who had actual notice, that is, direct information, of an unrecorded interest, have a lesser claim.

b. Possession: By taking possession of a property, an individual gives notice to the world that he has an interest in it, even if the deed is not recorded. It is the duty of a prospective buyer to find out what that interest is. If the buyer obtains and records a deed without inspecting the property, she has a lesser claim to it than the person possessing it does.

3. In order for a deed to be recorded, many states require that it be acknowledged by the Grantor in front of a notary public who witnesses the acknowledgment.

D. Elements necessary for the valid execution of a deed:

a. Signed and acknowledged by grantor(s)

b. Must show marital status of the grantor and spouse sign away dower rights

c. Use words of conveyance showing intention to convey (also called a "granting clause" e.g., "I grant, I give, I bequeath")

d. Names and address of grantees

e. Acknowledged by Grantor in front of a Notary Public

f. Signed in front of two witnesses (not in all states)

g. Legal description. Three types of legal descriptions: 1. metes and bounds, 2. government rectangular survey (NE ¼ of SE ¼ of SW ¼), and 3. lots and blocks (recorded plat of a subdivision)

h. Delivery and acceptance of deed

Types of Legal Description:

1. Lot and Block System:

   a. A subdivision is divided into blocks and lots; e.g., Lots 7 and 8 Block 4 of Hartley subdivision

   b. Because all states use this method, a description of such property must include the county and state, to distinguish it from the same description in another area

   c. Areas within a subdivision may be re-subdivided

2. Metes and Bounds. From a point of beginning (POB), measurement proceeds around the perimeter of the parcel. The description uses feet and degrees. Measurement must return to the point of beginning.

3. Rectangular (Government) Survey: Used in states west of the Ohio River.

   a. Measurements are based on principal meridians (lines running north-south) and base lines (lines running east-west)

   b. A township is 36 square miles (6 miles x 6 miles)

   c. There are 36 sections in a township; each one is a square mile. Sections are numbered, beginning with No. 1 in the northeast corner, going west and east, and section No. 36 ends in the southeast corner. **Section 16 is the school section.** Each section contains 640 acres; each acre contains 43,560 square feet

   d. The description may pinpoint locations by referring to quarters and halves within a section; e.g., SW ¼ of NE ¼. (Hint—always read legal description backwards to locate.)

ALL 36 SECTIONS IN ONE TOWNSHIP

1 MILE | 6 MILES (36 SQ. MILES)

6	5	4	3	2	1
7	8	9	10	11	12
18	17	SCHOOL 16 SECTION	15	14	13
19	20	21	22	23	24
30	29	28	27	26	25
31	32	33	34	35	36

1 MILE (left side), 6 MILES (left side)

ONE SECTION

640 ACRES   **5,280 FEET = 1 MILE**

ONE SECTION

640 ACRES

5280 FEET = 1 MILE

2640'

1 MILE

1320'

1320'

1320'

W ½
OF NW ¼
(80 ACRES)

1320'

E ½
OF NW ¼
(80 ACRES)

2640'

NE ¼
(160 ACRES)

NW ¼ OF SW ¼
(40 ACRES)

NE ¼ OF SW ¼
(40 ACRES)

N ½ OF NW ¼
OF SE ¼
(20 ACRES)

W ½
OF NE ¼
OF SE ¼
(20
ACRES)

(20 ACRES)

SW ¼ OF SW ¼
(40 ACRES)

(40 ACRES)

10
ACRES

10 ACRES

10 ACRES

5 acres

5 acres

5
ACRES

5

SE ¼
OF SE
¼ OF
SE ¼
10
ACRES

1 MILE

E. A street address is not a legal description.

F. Courts deem it to be a legal description if a licensed surveyor can locate it.

G. Legal descriptions should only be prepared by a surveyor or an attorney.

H. Other Terms to Remember
1. Datum: An imaginary line from which heights are measured.
2. Benchmark: The reference point used to measure elevation.
3. Government Lot: An undersized or fractional section.
4. Air Lot: A space over a given parcel of land.

I. Recording the deed does not make it legal. You only record the deed to give notice to the world of the interest you are receiving.

J. Having a deed notarized does not make it legal.
1. A deed is notarized to help ensure the identity of the grantors, and that they have acknowledged and signed as their voluntary act.
2. It is also a necessary element to having it recorded with the county recorder's office to give constructive notice to the world.

V. Transfer of Marketable Title

A. Voluntary alienation:
1. By gift
2. By sale

B. By involuntary alienation or involuntary taking: The owner does not consent to the property transfer.
1. Eminent Domain: This empowers the government authorities to condemn and take the property. Eminent domain is the right; condemnation is the process.
    a. The taking must be for the public benefit, e.g., to build a freeway.
    b. The taking authority must pay just compensation to the owner.
    c. Due process must be followed.
2. Foreclosure and Sale: The property is sold to pay delinquent taxes or the mortgage note.
3. Escheat: The state takes property upon the owner's death if no will exists and no heirs can be found. Also applies to abandoned properties.
4. Adverse Possession:
    a. A person takes possession of and uses property belonging to another. Possession must be open, notorious, hostile, and uninterrupted for a state-specified length of time.
    b. Under state law, the person who satisfies the requirements of adverse possession takes ownership, and the original owner loses rights to the property. Actual record title can only be established by court action.

C. By Will (Estate), or Transfer by Devise:
1. The owner of the property specifies who will inherit it at the time of his or her death.
2. The will, however, is subject to state laws that give the surviving spouse rights of dower, courtesy, or the option to take against the will.

D. By Descent: When a person dies without a will (intestate), state statute determines how the property will be divided. Usually, the decedent's closest living relatives inherit the property.

VI. Proof of Title (Title Evidence)

A. Types of Title Evidence:

 1. Abstract of Title: a complete history of ownership. An attorney searches the abstract for flaws and gives his opinion as to ownership. This opinion is called a Lawyer's Opinion Letter.

   a. Abstract does not pass judgment or guarantee condition of title.

   b. Opinion letter does not cover hidden defects of title (e.g., forgeries).

 2. Title Insurance: An insurance policy that indemnifies the holder against certain defects, for example, defects in public record, hidden defects (forgery), or defective transfers.

   a. Standard policies exclude coverage against such situations as unrecorded documents, defects the policyholder has knowledge of, questions of survey, and persons in possession.

   b. There are several types of title insurance policies:

     1) Mortgagee policy based on loan amount, which protects only the lender, not the owner (most lenders require it).

     2) Owner's fee policy based on purchase price, which protects the owner against "hidden defects" of the past. A mortgagee's policy can be simultaneously issued at a substantial savings.

     3) Title Guaranty is a combination of an abstract and title opinion.

     4) Leasehold policy insures lessee that they have a valid lease.

 3. Torrens System: a form of land registration using signature cards

   a. An Owner's Duplicate of Certificate of Title is filed with the registrar's office, along with the owner's signature.

   b. This information is used to verify future transfers. When exact duplicate of original certificate called owner's duplicate certificate is made and delivered instead of a deed. Eliminates the need for title searches.

VII. Other Interests and Items Affecting Real Estate

Items that affect marketability of title:

A. Encumbrance: A claim or liability that attaches to the land and is held by one who is not the fee owner. Types of encumbrances are liens, affecting title, and physical encumbrance, affecting land use.

 1. Liens: Charges against property as security for debt. The property may still be conveyed, but it is a risk for the buyer. Priority is usually determined by the order in which liens attach; earlier ones have priority.

   a. Specific liens: Liens on specific property.

     1. Real estate taxes, including general taxes and special assessment, have priority over all other liens.

     2. Mortgages

     3. Mechanic's lien is effective from the date that work began, not from the date the lien was filed. In most cases, workers must give notice and/or file a claim to obtain a lien. In some cases, a subcontractor can obtain a lien even if the property owner has paid the contract.

   b. General Liens: These liens apply to all the debtor's property, (e.g., IRS liens, judgments, or court decrees awarding money to the successful party in a lawsuit).

2. Encumbrances affecting the physical use of the land.

   a. Easement: The right to use property for specific purposes.

      1. Easement in Gross: This pertains to an entity's personal right to use property. Person receiving easement does not own adjoining property (e.g., utility companies, phone company).

      2. Easement Appurtenant: The easement runs with the land. Adjacent properties to this easement are dominant tenement (the tract of land benefiting from the easement) and servient tenement (the tract over which the easement runs).

      3. Easement by Necessity: This is created when no other access to land exists. Usually arises in the sale of inaccessible land (right of ingress and regress).

      4. Easement by Prescription: This is created through continual use over a certain period of time (prescriptive period). The use must be continual, visible, and without approval. A private road may become a public street in this manner.

   b. Creation of easements may occur by express grant, by reserving in deed, by implication, or by longtime usage.

√ **Note:** A phrase to remember: While all liens are encumbrances, not all encumbrances are liens.

B. License: An individual has the privilege to enter land for a specific purpose. A license cannot be assigned to others. This differs from easement in that it may be terminated at any time by the licensor. Examples of license are parking a car in a neighbor's driveway or giving someone permission to hunt on your property.

C. Encroachment: A building or other structure extends onto a neighbor's property, e.g., trees, fences, and driveways, etc.

D. Water Rights: Owners along waterways have the right to use the water as long as they do not interrupt the flow or pollute it.

   1. Riparian Rights: Rights of the owner along a river or stream

      a. Along navigable waters, owners possess land to the water's edge; the state owns submerged land and filled land.

      b. Along non-navigable waters, owners possess land to the center of the stream.

      c. Only land, not water, is owned.

      d. Remember that in some states, a Riparian owner owns to the middle of the river (for both navigable and non-navigable waters).

   2. Littoral Rights: Rights of owners along an ocean or large lake. Owners possess land to the high-water mark.

   3. Accretion: Physical addition to the land by natural forces.

   4. Erosion: Physical loss of land due to natural forces.

   5. Alluvium or Alluvion: The soil on a shore or bank of a river.

   6. Prior Appropriation: The right to use water is controlled by the state. An individual who wishes to use the water must indicate need and generally beneficial usage.

VIII. CONTROL OF LAND USE

Police power of states enables them to adopt regulations to protect the public health and welfare.

A. Police Powers Include:

1. Zoning

    a. Ordinances generally restrict the use of areas or regulate physical improvements. Ordinance restrictions may extend to such matters as density, building size, height, and minimum distance requirements.

    b. Zoning regulations classify land use as residential, commercial, industrial, or multiple-use.

    c. Non-conforming use: The use existed prior to the zoning restriction. The use is allowed to continue even though it does not meet zoning requirements.

    d. Variance: In situations where complying with an ordinance would cause hardship, a person may ask to be excused from complying.

2. Building Codes

3. Subdivision Regulations: Grading, sewers, etc.

4. Environmental Protection Legislation

5. Occupancy Permits

B. Private Land Use Control: Deed and declaration restrictions. For example, a dwelling must conform to the dimensions specified in the deed; often used to restrict the buyer's use of a property.

IX. Real Estate Taxes

These taxes take priority over all other liens against a property.

A. Ad Valorem Tax: Taxes are collectively levied on real estate by several governmental agencies and municipalities. The amount of tax is based on the value of the property.

1. Assessment: Real estate is assessed for tax purposes by county or township assessors.

2. Equalization: This factor corrects general inequities in statewide tax assessments.

3. Determination of Tax Rate:

    a. The taxing jurisdiction defines its needs and develops a budget.

    b. The assessed values of all properties within the local jurisdiction are computed.

    c. The appropriate tax rate is determined by dividing the total assessed values into the budget deficit.

    d. The tax rate is generally expressed in mills. One mill is 1/1000 of a dollar, or $0.001.

4. The tax bill is calculated by applying the tax rate to the assessed valuation of the property. Thus, a home with an assessed value for tax purposes of $30,000 multiplied by a tax rate of $3 per hundred dollars would generate a tax bill of $900.

B. Special assessments are special taxes levied on real estate that require property owners to pay for improvements that directly benefit the real estate they own, e.g., the installation of a sidewalk. They are not tax deductible.

X. Other Terms to Remember

A. Lis pendens: A notice filed before the conclusion of a lawsuit for the purpose of giving constructive notice of a possible claim to the property.

B. Writ of Attachment: A document filed during a lawsuit that prevents a debtor from conveying the property involved in the suit to someone else. Prevents debtor from hiding money.

C. State Documentary Stamps: Also known as transfer tax, conveyance fee, or auditor's tax: A fee to transfer property. Actual stamps are no longer used. The seller usually bears the cost of the stamps, which is based on the sales price.

D. Fixtures: Items of personal property that have been affixed to real property and are not removed by the seller. However, trade fixtures used in a business constitute personal property and can be removed by the lessee when the lease terminates.

E. Quiet Title Action: An action brought to cure a cloud on title to property.

F. Cloud on Title: A claim that makes clear ownership uncertain for the property in question.

Real Estate Valuation

I. The Concept of Value

A. An appraisal is an estimate or opinion of value.

B. Characteristics that comprise value are:

1. Demand		**D**
2. Utility		**U**
3. Scarcity	=	**S**
4. Transferability		**T**
5. Anticipation		**A**
6. Highest and Best Use		**H**

C. Types of Value: Real estate may have different values at the same time, e.g., market value, assessed value, mortgage value, and depreciated value.

D. Market Value vs. Market Price:

1. Market value is an estimate of probable price on the date of appraisal.

2. Market price is what the property actually sells for.

II. The Three Approaches to Value

A. Market Data Approach (primarily single-family): An estimate of value is obtained by comparing the subject property with recently sold, comparable properties.

B. Cost Approach (primarily commercial and industrial property): An estimate value is ascertained by determining the cost to replace or reproduce the structure. After replacement cost is determined, the depreciation of present structure is deducted to arrive at value. Depreciation can be:

1. Physical Deterioration (curable): Repairs, when made, are economically feasible, e.g., routine maintenance.

2. Physical Deterioration (incurable): Repairs to separate structural components that deteriorate at different rates, e.g., roof, electric system.

3. Functional Obsolescence (curable): Features of the structure no longer desirable by purchasers, but are replaceable, e.g., outmoded plumbing fixtures.

4. Functional Obsolescence (incurable): Undesirable physical or design features not easily replaceable, e.g., office building that cannot be air-conditioned.

5. Economic Obsolescence (incurable only): Caused by factors not on subject property, e.g., proximity to nuisance, pig farm, polluting factory.

C. Income Approach (primarily income producing property): The value is determined by analyzing the present worth of future income stream.

1. The formula for computation is:

$$\frac{\text{NET INCOME}}{\text{CAPITALIZATION RATE}} = \text{VALUE}$$

Formulas:

1. Value   x   Rate   =   Income
2. Income   ÷   Value   =   Rate
3. Income   ÷   Rate   =   Value

2. Gross Monthly Rent Multiplier (GMRM): A method of arriving at a rough estimate of value for income-producing residential properties primarily purchased for income. On the state exam, GMRM problems are always stated as ANNUAL Gross Income problems. The formulas are:

1. Gross Rent Income   x   Multiplier   =   Sales Price
2. Sales Price   ÷   Gross Rent Income   =   Multiplier
3. Sales Price   ÷   Multiplier   =   Gross Rents

D. Reconciliation: The final step in the appraisal process where the appraiser reconciles the estimates of value from sales comparison, cost, and income approaches to arrive at the final estimate of market value for subject property. Appraisers never average!

THE APPRAISAL PROCESS

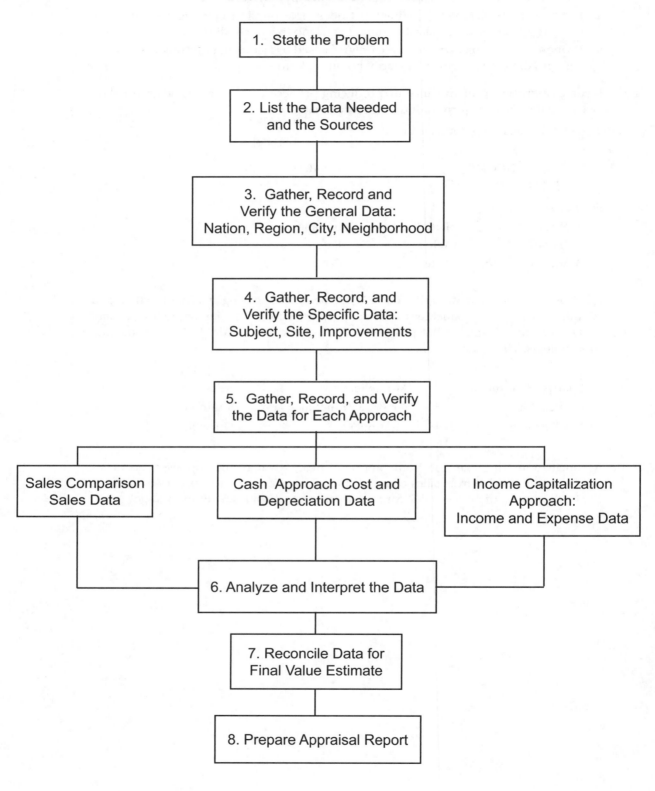

1. State the Problem

2. List the Data Needed
and the Sources

3. Gather, Record and
Verify the General Data:
Nation, Region, City, Neighborhood

4. Gather, Record, and
Verify the Specific Data:
Subject, Site, Improvements

5. Gather, Record, and Verify
the Data for Each Approach

Sales Comparison
Sales Data

Cash Approach Cost and
Depreciation Data

Income Capitalization
Approach:
Income and Expense Data

6. Analyze and Interpret the Data

7. Reconcile Data for
Final Value Estimate

8. Prepare Appraisal Report

Property Management

Manager Responsibilities

There are three types of managers to be aware of:

1. Property manager: Oversees the management of a number of properties for various owners

2. Building manager: Is involved in the management of one building

3. Resident manager: Represents a property management firm (and may live on the premises of the building that he or she manages)

The functions of the manager are:

- Develop a management plan that incorporates the owner's purpose
- Lease space
- Select tenants
- Collect rents
- Tenant relations
- Maintain and repair the property
- Prepare and execute the budget

Covenant of Quiet Enjoyment A guarantee that a tenant has the right to exclusive, undisturbed possession of a leasehold estate, and will not be disturbed by the previous owner, the lessor, or anyone else claiming an interest in the property.

Triple Net A lease where the tenant pays the operating expenses of the property, and a proportion of the expenses of the shared or common spaces.

Rent Control Government restrictions on how much rent a landlord can charge. These are usually local ordinances, only enacted in a few communities.

Lease/Option When a seller leases property to someone for a specific term with an option to buy the property at a predetermined price during the lease term, usually with a portion of the lease payments applied toward the purchase price. The option gives a tenant the right, but not the obligation, to buy the property.

Sublease When a tenant transfers only part of the tenant's right of possession or other interest in leased property to another person for part of the remaining lease term. This is different than an assignment, where the tenant gives up possession for the entire remainder of the lease term.

Tenancy at Sufferance Possession of property by a holdover tenant.

Holdover Tenant A lessee who remains in possession of property after a lease has expired; a tenant who refuses to surrender possession of property at lease's end.

Notice to Vacate A notice to a tenant, demanding the tenant vacate the leased property. Also called a "notice to quit." The first step in the eviction process.

Writ of Execution Court order directing a public officer (often the sheriff or marshal) to seize and/or sell property to regain possession for the owner and/or satisfy a debt. Also called a "writ of ejectment." The last step in the eviction process.

Constructive Eviction When a landlord's act (or failure to act) interferes with the tenant's quiet enjoyment of the property, or makes the property unfit for its intended use, to such an extent that the tenant is forced to move out.

Self-Help Eviction When a landlord uses physical force, a lockout, or a utility shut-off to get rid of a tenant, instead of the legal process. (Not legal in most states.)

Retaliatory Eviction When a landlord evicts a tenant in retaliation for complaining about code violations or violations of law, or for joining a tenants' rights group. (Not legal in most states.)

Exculpatory Clause A clause in a contract or lease providing that one of the parties will not be liable in the event the other party (or someone else) is injured. This type of clause is void in residential leases in many states.

Real Estate Development The process of acquiring large tracts of land at a low cost per acre, then subdividing and improving it with streets, sewers, and utilities so it can be resold at a higher cost per front foot (for lots) or per square foot (for buildings). Land can be developed for residential, commercial, industrial, or other uses, often with the help of a management company.

- Safeguard the owner's interests in tenant/employee/building matters
- Supervise all building personnel
- Record keeping (income and expenditures)

Property managers have an agency relationship with property owners and thus, owe fiduciary duties of accountability, care, confidentiality, obedience, loyalty and disclosure (ACCOLD) to the principal. Property managers are general agents. A license is required in most states to take a listing, publish a listing, negotiate a lease, and interact with *potential* tenants. Unlicensed personnel can interact with tenants *after* they have leased a unit (e.g., collect rents, arrange for maintenance, etc.)

Property Management Trust Accounts: All brokerages that manage property for another brokerage shall establish and maintain a separate trust account, designated as the property management trust account.

- There must be sufficient funds credited to the owner's account to cover expenses that are paid from the property management trust account
- Security deposits must also be deposited into this account
- Property management trust accounts may be interest bearing. (Regular trust accounts held by real estate brokers may **not** be interest bearing.)
- Property management brokerages must provide an accounting of property managed to each owner on at least a quarterly basis.

Leases

Leases are both a conveyance of a leasehold estate from the fee owner to a tenant, and a contract in which one party pays the other rent in exchange for possession of the real estate. Leases are often called rental agreements. As a conveyance, a lease temporarily transfers the right of possession of property from the owner (the landlord or lessor). To another (the tenant or lessee). Although the landlord still owns the property in fee simple, the tenant has a leasehold estate. As a contract, a lease states the terms of the parties' relationship.

Let's review the basic leasehold estates:

- *Estate for Years*: A lease valid for a fixed period of time—*any* fixed period of time, not just years. Also called *term tenancy*.
- *Periodic Tenancy*: A lease that is not limited to a specific term, but continues from period to period, as agreed by the parties.
- *Tenancy at Will*: A lease with no specific termination date and no regular rental period. Sometimes no rent is paid, or rent is not based on time, e.g., percentage of sales. Prohibited in some states.

Requirements for a valid/enforceable lease are the same as those for a valid contract.

a. *Capacity*: competent, age of majority (18 years old in most states)

b. *Offer*: "intent to contract," definite terms for completion

c. *Acceptance*: no alteration of terms, "meeting of the minds"

d. *Consideration*: each party must give something of value

e. *Lawful and possible objective*: illegal provisions may be severable

f. *Must be in writing* if it's for more than one year. In some states, a lease for 3+ years must be attested, acknowledged, and recorded.

  (*Note*: only items b, c, and d are necessary for a valid lease; items a, e, and f are necessary to be enforceable in a court of law.)

Leases are classified by the method of rent payment.

a. *Gross lease*: Tenant pays fixed amount of rent and landlord pays the expenses. This is a typical residential lease.

b. *Net lease*: Tenant pays expenses—taxes, insurance, maintenance—in addition to a fixed rent. A typical commercial lease.

c. *Percentage lease*: Tenant pays a percentage of gross sales (not from profit) that the business earns from the property as rent. This arrangement is often used in shopping centers.

d. *Ground lease*: A long-term lease of land (e.g., 99 years). During the term of the lease, the tenant usually operates the property as though it were tenant-owned and may construct buildings on it.

e. *Variable lease*: Rent changes periodically during the lease term. The amount of change could be specified in the lease or depend on an outside index such as the Consumer Price Index (CPI).

Other points to know about leases:

•   If a new lease is not signed once a lease expires, an estate for years becomes a periodic tenancy

•   A buyer of leased property takes it subject to the existing leases, unless the leases provide otherwise (or the leases are not recorded)

•   Assignment or subleasing is generally allowed unless the lease forbids it or places conditions on it

•   If there is an assignment or sublease, the original tenant is still liable for any default in the rent

Ways a lease can be terminated:

1. *Surrender*: giving up an estate before it expires. If landlord and tenant mutually agree, then the tenant owes no more rent.

2. *Destruction of the building*: the lease's purpose is frustrated if a building is damaged or destroyed, so the tenancy ends with no more rent due.

3. *Eviction*: dispossessing or expelling someone from real property. Valid reasons for eviction vary by state, but non-payment of rent or breach of another duty under the lease terms are common reasons.

4. *Abandonment*: failure to occupy and use property. Landlord may still sue for rent owed or other damages.

Landlords and Tenants

Landlord and tenant laws vary by state. Many states make a distinction between how commercial tenants and residential tenants are treated under the law. Different standards apply and different rights are enjoyed by each type of tenant. The state-specific part of this textbook has some details. Here are some generalities:

•   Nonresidential leases are governed by caveat emptor (buyer beware) and the stated lease terms

•   Residential leases are governed by state laws giving landlords and tenants statutory duties and rights, many of which can't be waived

•   Nonresidential landlords must warn tenants of known latent defects, but don't have to put property into good condition

•   Residential landlords must make buildings fit for human habitation, and keep them fit during the tenancy

- Landlords for residential leases are required to comply with the lead-based paint disclosure rules. For houses built before 1978:
  a. Tenants must be given a lead paint brochure
  b. Known lead paint hazards must be disclosed
  c. Must give tenants a 10-day period to conduct lead tests

There are several liability issues when dealing with landlord/tenant law:

1. If a residential landlord doesn't make repairs as agreed, or within a reasonable time as required by law, the tenant may be able to pay rent to the court as custodian. The tenant is only liable for the reasonable rental value of the property in its substandard condition.

2. A landlord can keep a tenant's security deposit to cover unpaid rent or damage, but not for ordinary wear and tear. A residential landlord must give an itemized explanation if the full deposit isn't returned.

3. Tort liability for injuries is based on negligence. If a landlord had a duty to repair something, the landlord may be held liable for injuries that occur.
   a. Tort actions look at four elements: duty, breach, injury, causation. The elements must occur in that order from a legal standpoint. The person must have a duty to others, which is breached, and another is injured as a causation of the breach.
   b. The comparative negligence rule in tort law says that if a tenant (or other party) was partially responsible for the tort, then that party must also share a portion of the responsibility for damages.

4. A landlord can collect damages for lost rent if a tenant doesn't pay as agreed.
   a. If the tenant abandons the property, the landlord can sue for rent during the time the unit is vacant, until the end of the lease period. But the landlord has a duty to mitigate (lessen) the amount of damages by trying to find a new tenant as quickly as possible, rather than rely on getting the full amount from the tenant.
   b. If the tenant is evicted, the courts are split on whether the landlord can collect rent from ~~form~~ the tenant. Part of the question revolves around why the eviction occurred. Nevertheless, the landlord still has an obligation to try to mitigate damages.

Landlords violate the Federal Fair Housing Act if they reject a prospective tenant based on race, color, religion, sex, national origin, disability, or familial status—even if there are also other legitimate reasons for rejecting the tenant. State and local laws may add more protected classes.

Civil Rights

Questions regarding civil rights and discrimination laws should not be made difficult for exam purposes. There are only a few basic laws that we need to have a solid understanding of to answer all questions on the exam correctly. The primary thing to keep in mind when answering this type of question is that you must be **CONSERVATIVE**. Many of these questions are common-sense questions. Remember, the state is not going to try to keep you from finding ways to discriminate, for instance:

For Example

#1: Q. An out-of-towner says he wants an all-white neighborhood. How do you reply?

A. The safest answer is "I'm sorry. It is illegal for me to discuss those issues."

#2: Q. Buyers come in and ask you, "How's the school system?" How do you reply?

A. The safest way to answer is to never give your own opinion. If there are facts or statistics on schools prepared by others, that may be okay—ask your broker.

In being conservative, you must remember the only basis on which to discriminate legally is an economic basis, meaning that income or credit history can make prospective buyers unqualified for a particular purchase.

The primary laws to know for the exam are the following:

- Original Civil Rights Act of 1866
- Federal Fair Housing Act of 1968
- Jones v. Mayer (Supreme Court case decision) 1968
- Your state's Civil Rights Laws

Original Civil Rights Act of 1866

The original Civil Rights Act of 1866 basically stated that all citizens, whites and blacks, have the same rights to inherit, purchase, lease, hold, and convey real and/or personal property. In other words, when it comes to race, you could not discriminate in the sale or rental of housing or with regard to personal property.

Federal Fair Housing Laws

A. Civil Rights Act of 1866: This act prohibits all racial discrimination, public or private, in the sale or rental of all real or personal property. No exceptions!

B. Fair Housing Act of 1968: This law makes it unlawful to discriminate because of race, color, religion, sex, national origin, familial status, or disability in the sale or rental of real estate. (Disability and Familial Status Amendment 1988).

   1. Prohibited discrimination includes:
       a. refusing to sell, rent, or negotiate with any person
       b. changing the terms of a transaction for certain people
       c. discriminatory advertising
       d. wrongly representing that a house is unavailable
       e. blockbusting—inducing an owner to sell by representing that minorities will be moving into the neighborhood
       f. redlining—refusing to make loans or provide insurance to persons in certain areas, without regard to their qualifications
       g. steering—leading prospective homeowners to or away from certain areas based on race, creed, color, etc.
       h. denying membership in MLS services, real estate brokers' organization, or other facility related to the sale or rental of dwellings as a means of discrimination

   2. Exemptions from the law:
       a. The sale or rental of a single-family home
           1. which is owned by a person who does not own more than three other homes
           2. in which the owner is currently living, or was the most recent occupant
           3. for which no broker was used
           4. about which no discriminatory advertising was used
       b. The rental of a room or unit in an owner-occupied, 1–4 family dwelling
       c. Rooms owned by religious organizations may be restricted to persons of the same religion

    d. Private clubs' lodgings may be restricted to members, if the lodgings are not commercially operated

    e. Commercial and industrial real estate

  3. Fair Housing poster suggested by HUD is required by most state laws to be displayed in the broker's office.

  4. Besides the Federal Fair Housing Laws, there are each state's Fair Housing Laws which may or may not allow any or all exemptions.

Fair Housing Act of 1968

This was the primary legislative act that has had the greatest impact on housing and discrimination. The original Fair Housing Act of 1968 stated it was illegal to discriminate in the sale or rental of housing based on race, color, religion, or national origin, with certain exemptions or exceptions.

Sex was added to this act in 1974, as was familial status (families with children under 18), and disability in 1988. As of today, the Federal Fair Housing Act covers race, color, religion, sex, national origin, familial status, and disability.

The following were exempted under the Federal Fair Housing Act:

A. Single family homes, if owner-occupied, as long as no more than three such sales took place within a two-year period

B. An owner-occupied dwelling, if four or fewer units

C. Private clubs who let only their members rent or occupy rooms

D. Religious group permitting only members of its religion to rent or occupy its dwelling units, **as long as the religion did not restrict its membership on the basis of race or national origin**

Also note that the Americans with Disabilities Act (ADA) expanded the accommodations that must be made for disabled people as a means of prohibiting discrimination. One focus of the ADA is buildings designed to serve the public. All new construction as of Jan. 26, 1993 and all building renovations must be in compliance.

Jones v. Mayer – 1968

Jones v. Mayer was a landmark Supreme Court decision in that it reenacted the original Civil Rights Act of 1866. It stated that when it came to race in regard to the sale or rental of housing there were **no exceptions or exemptions.**

ANTI-DISCRIMINATION and FAIR HOUSING LAWS SUMMARIZED			
	Civil Rights Act of 1866	Federal Fair Housing Act	Federal Equal Credit Opportunity Act
Race	X	X	X
Color	X	X	X
Religion		X	X
Sex		X	X
National Origin		X	X
Ancestry	X		
Disability/Handicap		X	
Familial Status		X	
Age			X
Marital Status			X
Receipt of Public Assistance			X
All property (Real + Personal)	X		X
Only housing + land for housing		X	
Housing and ANY vacant land			
Exceptions		1. FSBO	
(FSBO = For Sale By Owner)	NONE	2. FSBO 4-plex	
		3. Religious Groups	
		4. Private Cllubs	
Statute of Limitations	Same as State	1 Year for HUD	
	(1 year in Ohio)	2 Years for Court	

Terms to Remember—*These will be on the test in one form or another!*

Blockbusting

An illegal act whereby owners are encouraged to sell their properties because minorities are moving into a neighborhood. It derives from racial fears that prey upon housing owners in a given area (block). Panic selling can be created by using tactics to start rumors that certain neighborhoods are going a certain way. The agent benefits from this panic. This is illegal under federal and state law. Also known as panic peddling.

Steering

The illegal practice of trying to influence a buyer's housing choice using racial, religious, ethnic, national origin, or ancestry factors. This includes showing only certain neighborhoods, or downgrading or slanting certain neighborhoods to influence minority buyers. This is illegal under federal and state law.

Redlining

The illegal practice of denying loans in certain areas of a community because of race, color, creed, religion, sex, national origin, familial status, and disability/disability. This occurs any time a decision is made that is not based on the buyers' qualifications. (It is also a practice used at times in the insurance industry.) This is illegal under federal and state law.

FAIR HOUSING INFORMATION

	Civil Rights Act of 1866	Fair Housing Act: Civil Rights Act of 1968 Title VIII As Amended by 1988 Fair Housing Act
What the Laws Say	**Grant all citizens the same rights with regard to property as white citizens.**	Prohibits discrimination in the sale, rental, lease, or negotiations for real property based on race, color, religion, sex, disability, familial status, or national origin. Also prohibits discrimination in financing or provision of brokerage services.
Whom the Laws Protect	**Grant all citizens the same rights with regard to property as white citizens.**	Protects all persons (citizens or non-citizens) affected by discriminatory practices.
The Penalties the Court can Order	Injunctive relief, compensatory and punitive damages. Attorney's fees to the successful plaintiff.	Injunctive relief, compensatory and punitive damages which are not limited by the statute. Attorneys' fees may be allowed by the court or administrative judge to successful plaintiffs. Fines can be levied: * Up to \$11,000 for first offense, \$27,500 for 2nd offense, * Up to \$55,000 for 3rd or more offenses w/in 7 years
The Amount of Time Available To File a Complaint	*Determined by state law*	*One year after an alleged discriminatory housing practice has occurred or terminated to file a complaint with HUD or two (2) years after occurrence or the termination of an alleged discriminatory housing practice to file the complaint in federal district court.*
Basis for Filing Fair Housing Complaints	Discrimination against non-white citizens. Discrimination in the sale or rental of any type of property.	Discrimination based on race, color, religion, sex, disability, familial status, or national origin. Discrimination in the sale or rental of a dwelling.
How the Laws Are Enforced	**Civil actions can be brought in state or federal courts by persons injured by discriminatory conduct prohibited by the Act.**	The Attorney General can enforce this law where a "pattern or practice" of discrimination can be shown or where the issue presented is of general public importance. A person injured by an allegedly discriminatory practice can file a complaint with HUD or may file a suit in federal court without regard to the amount of damages in controversy. The secretary of HUD, on the secretary's own initiative, may file a complaint with HUD alleging a discriminatory housing practice. **Hearings on complaints filed with HUD may be transferred to the federal court for hearing in a civil action if requested by any party within twenty (20) days of receipt of service by the electing party.**
Types of Situations NOT Covered by the Laws	*No Exclusions*	Boarding houses with no more than three units and owner occupied. Transactions that do not involve the use of a broker or agent. **Noncommercial private clubs.**

I. Law Of Agency

A. Broker is an agent of the principal.

B. Principal may be an owner, lessor, tenant, seller, or buyer of property. The broker owes fiduciary duty to the principal.

C. The principal may be a prospective buyer or seller of a property. Even though brokers owe a fiduciary duty to the principal, the broker is obligated to disclose all facts concerning a property to other parties to a transaction. It's the seller's responsibility to reveal any latent defects to the buyer. In some states, *caveat emptor* (buyer beware) applies to real estate sales, but only as to obvious defects.

D. The real estate broker is a special agent; that is, one who works for a principal on one specific transaction only. Brokers are authorized to negotiate contracts, but have no power to buy or sell property, or to bind the principal to a contract.

E. To be entitled to a brokerage fee, a broker must (by statute):

1. Be licensed during the period of agency.
2. Be employed by a principal under a listing contract or buyer broker agreement.
3. Act in good faith.

F. It is illegal for a broker to share a fee with someone not licensed, if that fee is compensation for an act that requires a real estate license.

G. Dual agency (one broker representing both the buyer and seller in a single transaction) is prohibited unless the broker has obtained both parties' prior consent in writing.

H. The broker must not act as an agent and undisclosed party to the transaction. Any personal interest in property must be made known to and accepted by the other party.

I. The broker must not receive profits, fees, or rebates from a transaction without the consent of the principal.

J. The broker must present all offers to the principal.

K. The broker must have a fixed place of business.

L. The broker must keep a non-interest-bearing trust account for all money in the broker's possession belonging to others, except funds received in a property management activity, which then must be placed in an appropriate property management trust account, which may bear interest.

M. Most states prohibit placing blind ads; that is, advertisements that do not indicate the broker is the advertiser. Ads placed by salespersons must also identify their employing broker by name. The broker's name needs to be equal to or greater in prominence than the salesperson's name.

N. Unless the consent of the listing broker is obtained, all negotiations must take place through the listing broker rather than directly with the owner.

II. Salesperson

A. The salesperson acts on behalf of the broker. Salesperson is an agent of the broker; salesperson is a subagent of the client.

B. The salesperson has no direct relationship with the principal, but is only responsible to the broker.

C. The salesperson may be either an employee of the broker or an independent contractor working under the broker, but is usually an independent contractor.

III. Ethical Considerations

A. Fraud: Puffing versus Fraud

    1. Puffing—an opinion or the exaggeration of the property's benefits.

    2. Fraud—intentional misrepresentation of facts.

B. Violations of antitrust laws (Sherman Antitrust Act)

    1. Price fixing—brokers conspire to receive the same fee for services.

    2. Allocation of the market—brokers conspire to restrict competition by dividing the market into exclusive areas of operation. For example, the market may be allocated by geography or by the price of the home.

C. REALTOR® Code of Ethics – Applies to members only (not on state exam).

    1. Applies toward the general public.

    2. Applies toward clients.

    3. Applies toward fellow brokers.

    4. Requires specific NAR ethics training not satisfied by some states' license law requirements for continuing education.

D. Each state may also have its own Code or Canon of Ethics.

IV. Types Of Listing Agreements

A. Open Listing:

    1. Any number of brokers may be retained. The broker who sells the property receives the commission.

    2. If the owner finds a buyer, no broker receives a commission.

B. Exclusive Agency Listing:

    1. Only one broker is authorized to sell.

    2. If the owner finds a buyer, the broker does not receive a commission.

C. Exclusive-Right-to-Sell Listing:

    1. Only one broker is authorized to sell.

    2. If anyone finds a buyer, the broker still receives a commission during the term of agency.

D. Net Listing:

    1. The broker's commission is whatever amount is received above a quoted net price.

    2. This arrangement is frowned upon by most states, and outlawed by some.

V. Other Broker Services

A. Guaranteed Sale Plan: The broker agrees to buy a house if not sold within a specified time for a specified minimum price. The broker's purchase price is the minimum price.

B. Multiple Listing Service:

    1. Brokers formally exchange information on listings.

    2. Commissions are split between the listing and selling brokers, according to the individual agreement between them.

    3. Commissions are negotiable:

        a. between the seller and broker

        b. between brokers

VI. Types Of Brokers

A. Real Estate Broker engages in the sale of real estate.

1. Agent in sale of real estate

2. Acts on behalf of principal

3. Regulated by state statutes

B. Securities Broker engages in the sale of stocks, bonds, and other security investments.

1. Regulated by Federal Securities Act 1933 and state Blue-Sky laws

2. Agent in the sale of securities

3. Exempt from real estate license laws in the sale of real estate

4. Sales of real estate investment trusts (REITS)

C. Mortgage Broker engages in the sale of real estate loans to secondary market lenders (Fannie Mae, Freddie Mac, Ginny Mae)

1. Agent in sale of loans secured by real property

2. Acts on behalf of lender

3. Regulated by state statutes

VII. Property Management

A. Types of Managers (typically termed a "general agent")

1. Property Manager: Oversees the management of a number of properties for various owners.

2. Building Manager: Involved in the management of one building.

3. Resident Manager: Represents a property management firm; typically, lives on the premises managed.

B. Functions of the Property Manager:

1. Develop management plan that incorporates the owner's purpose.

2. Collect rents.

3. Maintain the property.

4. Prepare and execute the budget.

5. Safeguard owner's interests in tenant/employee/building matters.

6. Lease space.

7. Record keeping.

Classification of leases by method of rent payment.

1) Gross Lease: Tenant pays fixed rent amount and landlord pays expenses (typical residential lease).

2) Net Lease: Tenant pays expenses (taxes, insurance, and/or maintenance) in addition to a fixed rent (typical commercial lease).

3) Percentage Lease: The tenant pays a percentage of gross sales (not from profit) that he earns from the property as rent. This arrangement is often used in shopping centers.

4) Ground Lease: A long-term lease of land (e.g., 99 years). During the term of the lease, the tenant usually operates the property as though it were tenant-owned and may construct buildings on it.

5) Variable Lease: Rent changes periodically during the lease term. The amount of change could be specified in the lease or depend on an outside index such as the Consumer Price Index.

Math Review

6

INDEX

I. Introduction to Math and Analysis of Real Estate Problems

A. Using a Calculator

While taking the Real Estate Exam, it is recommended that you use a hand-held calculator to perform the needed calculations. More time and risks are assumed by doing the required calculations by hand. If a calculator must be purchased, avoid solar-powered calculators, due to possible insufficient light. Also, avoid complex ones, since the most important factor is familiarity with the calculator's usage.

The explanations in this book are presented in the sequence of the calculations on a **hand-held** calculator. The symbols for mathematical operations are defined as follows:

+	Press the add key
-	Press the subtract key
x	Press the multiply key
÷	Press the divide key
=	Press the equals key

NOTE: A Hewlett-Packard calculator requires different key operations for the data entry and math functions.

By entering numbers and pressing mathematical operations in the proper sequence, problems can be solved without having to find common denominators and other advanced mathematical concepts. All you need for the State Exam is a process of translating English words into calculator language.

For example: What is 144 divided by 640?

Display on Calculator

Enter	144	144
Press	÷	144.0000
Enter	640	640
Press	=	0.2250

This book will present the above in this form: 144 ÷ 640 = 0.2250

The **ENTER** and **PRESS** are implied not stated. The answer on the calculator reads 0.2250. It is actually 22.5%. It is standard for an answer to be converted from decimal to percentage. The method is to move the decimal 2 places to the right or multiply the calculator answer by 100. If a problem contains a percent, it should be converted to decimal for the calculator by moving the invisible decimal on the right 2 places to the left or by dividing by 100.

Hints

When using a calculator for the Real Estate Exam, some helpful hints are:

1. Set the calculator if possible to **show four (4) decimal places**—that is 0.0000

2. If your calculator has a memory or multiple storage registers, information such as value of Pi, the number of acres in a section, etc., can be stored for later use.

Calculator examples:

Example 1.1: What is 80% of 225?

$$80 \div 100 \ \times \ 225 = 180 \ \text{ or } \ 80 \ (\% \text{ key}) \ \times \ 225 = 180$$

NOTE: The first division of 80 by 100 converts a percent to a decimal fraction. "OF" means times.

Example 1.2: What is one-quarter of 640 divided by 4?

$$1 \div 4 \ \times \ 640 \div 4 \ = \ 40$$

NOTE: "One-quarter" translates to math symbols as ¼ which translates into calculator language as 1 ÷ 4. The fraction is a division problem. After translating, this problem is solved from left to right.

When we multiply numbers, we can enter them into the calculator in any order.

Example: 3 x 5 x 6 is the same as 5 x 3 x 6. We can also mix multiplication and division steps when doing a chain of calculations. Example: 3 x 4 ÷ 2 ÷ 3 x 6 is the same as 3 x 4 x 6 ÷ 2 ÷ 3. Sometimes when we calculate acreage, we have this type of problem.

Example: 640 x ¼ x ½ x ¾ can be entered into the calculator most easily as 640 x 3 ÷ 4 ÷ 2 ÷ 4, but could have been done as 640 ÷ 4 ÷ 2 x 3 ÷ 4 (notice we do not bother multiplying or dividing by 1 since we would get the same answer).

The percent key is the last key we use in a calculation and must be immediately preceded by the percent number. Example: 7% of 29,500 can be written as 0.07 x 29,500 and entered into the calculator that way. However, if you wish to multiply by 7%, you must enter the numbers into the calculator as 29,500 x 7%, where the % key is pushed last and do not push the = key.

Exceptions can be found to this value with a very few calculators. Try your calculator to become familiar with exactly how it operates.

B. Fractions, Decimals, and Percentages to Other Equivalents

Conversion of fractions, decimals, and percentages to other equivalents:

¼ is converted to a decimal by dividing one by four 1 ÷ 4 = 0.25

0.25 is said to be the decimal equivalent of ¼

Examples:

1/2 = 0.50	2/3 = 0.666	9/5 = 1.80
3/4 = 0.75	1 1/4 = 1.25	1 9/5 = 2.80
7/8 = 0.875	5 7/8 = 5.875	32/8 = 4.00

Rounding up and down and rounding off:

Sometimes your calculator will show an answer to six or eight decimal places:
1 ÷ 3 = 0.33333333

To **round off** to two decimal places, drop all numbers after the second number to the right of the decimal. (0.33333333 rounds off to 0.33 or 0.66666666 rounds off to 0.66).

To **round up** or **round down** (half adjust), look at the first number we intend to drop and make an adjustment to the last number we intend to keep based on the number to be dropped. If the number to be dropped is five or greater, we adjust the last number by one. If the number is less than five, we just drop it off without an adjustment.

Examples of rounding (half adjusting): Rounding to two decimal places we look at the 3rd number and adjust the second.

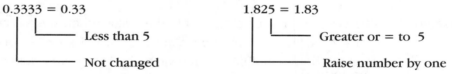

0.3333 = 0.33   Less than 5   Not changed

1.825 = 1.83   Greater or = to 5   Raise number by one

When rounding to three decimal places, we look at the fourth number and adjust the third.

3.1416 = 3.142	16.16149 = 16.161
Greater or = to 5	Less than 5
Raise number by one	Not changed

C. Calculator Logic

Look at your answer and ask yourself if it makes sense. Some basic rules follow:

1. If you divide a number by a number less than one, your answer will always be a larger number than you started with. Example: 6 ÷ 0.5 = 12

2. When you multiply a number by a percent less than 100%, your answer must be a smaller number.

   (Example: 420 x 75% = 315) When you multiply by percents larger than 100%, your answer must be a larger number.

3. Write down the number from your calculator if you are confused by what you see. Put the decimals and commas in the proper place. Remember to put commas so as to divide numbers left of the decimal into groups of three, starting at the decimal. If the number looks right except for the decimal place, that is a clue that you did not enter the (%) properly or convert to decimals properly.

Example: What I wanted was: $350 \times 15\% = 52.5$

What I may have done: $350 \times 15 = 5,250$

4. If the choices are in fractions, you must change them to decimal form or percents since your calculator will give you only those two forms of answers.

Example: 12 is what portion of 100?

First we can divide 12 by 100: $12 \div 100 = 0.12$, then convert answers to decimal form.

(a) 1/8 $(1 \div 8 = 0.125)$ (b) 3/25 $(3 \div 25 = 0.120)$

(c) 1/12 $(1 \div 12 = 0.083)$ (d) 2/9 $(2 \div 9 = 0.222)$

D. Number Logic

A basic rule of math says that we can divide both sides of an equation by the same number and still have equality. A simple equation means a simple formula.

Examples of equalities: $3 \times 2 = 6$

We could divide both sides of this equation by 2 and still have an equality.

Proof: $\dfrac{3 \times 2^1}{2_1} = \dfrac{6^3}{2_1}$ $\dfrac{^1 3 \times 2}{^1 3} = \dfrac{6^2}{3^1}$

$3 \times 1 = 3$ is an equality   (We could also divide both sides
by 3; $1 \times 2 = 2$ is an equality)

Simple Equation: $3 \times (?) = 12$

We can divide both sides by 3: $\dfrac{3 \times ?}{3} =$ or $\dfrac{12}{3}$ $? = \dfrac{12}{3} = 4$

Let's take a simple formula such as: $A \times B = C$ or $C = A \times B$

If we divide both sides by A: (review number logic)

$\dfrac{A \times B}{A} = \dfrac{C}{A}$ or $B = \dfrac{C}{A}$

If we divide both sides by B:

$\dfrac{A \times B}{B} = \dfrac{C}{B}$ or $A = \dfrac{C}{B}$

The pie tells us when to divide or when to multiply. It is easy to see that if we know two out of the three parts to this simple formula, we can calculate the third part by either multiplying or dividing.

Word Problem Logic

The challenge in word problems is first to decide what you are looking for and, second, the relevance of the information that was given. A couple of key words are "is" and "of."

Example: One-fourth of the appraised value is the assessed value of $12,000. How much was the house appraised for?

Solution:

Key ===>	One-fourth	of	Appraised value	is	Assessed Value
Equation ===>	1/4	x	?	=	$12,000
or	25%	x	?	=	$12,000

	?	=	$\dfrac{\$12,000}{0.25}$	=	$48,000

or	25%	x	?	=	$12,000

	?	=	$\dfrac{\$12,000}{25\%}$	=	$48,000

Notice that two out of the three pieces of the formula were given in the problem.

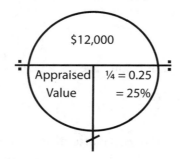 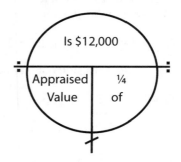

E. Percentages

A percentage is a way of expressing the relationship between a part and its whole. Fifty cents is 50% of a dollar: 50 cents is a part of a whole dollar. Another way of saying the same thing is one half (½) of a dollar is fifty cents (50 cents) or even 0.5 dollars is fifty cents.

For example:

1/2	=	0.5	=	50% of 1
1/4	=	0.25	=	25% of 1
1/8	=	0.125	=	12.5% of 1
2	=	2.0	=	200% of 1

You can see that we can express a decimal number in the form of a percent by moving the decimal two places to the right. If there is only one decimal place existing, or no decimal places, simply add zeroes to the right.

Examples:

0.1	=	0.10	=	10%
		0.25	=	25%
		0.125	=	12.5%
		0.1618	=	16.18%
1	=	1.00	=	100%
2.3	=	2.30	=	230%

Remember, percents relate to some portion of one (1) whole thing—100% is the *whole* thing; 50% is *half* the whole thing; 200% is *double* the whole thing.

When the whole is as simple as one dollar, the percentages of 25%, 50%, etc., are easily understood. Now let's talk "wholes," for example, one house, one parcel of land, one apartment complex.

We now use percentages to express the part of the home each person owns, the part of the sales price for the home that will be paid to the real estate sales person as a commission.

F. Multiplication

Multiplying is a short cut to adding something to itself over and over again. Three times five is the same as five plus five plus five. This process is simplified very much with a calculator.

G. Division

Dividing one number by another is a way to decide how many of that size part make up the whole. Division is the reverse process of multiplication. Fifteen divided by five is three, or how many fives make fifteen. This process can get complicated…but not with a calculator.

If we multiply fractions such as 1/4 x 3/8 x 7/16, we can multiply the top numbers to get one top number (numerator) and multiply the bottom numbers to get one bottom number (denominator). The above problem can be written as (1 x 3 x 7) ÷ (4 x 8 x 16) or 21/512.

Next, let's consider dividing one fraction by another. Example: 1/3 ÷ 3/4. The rule is simple! *Invert* the fraction you are to *divide by* and multiply. 1/3 x 4/3 = 4/9

H. Solving Simple Equations (Formulas)

For all our math problems, we can write simple equations consisting of three parts. In every problem, two out of three parts of the equation must be given.

Sometimes the problem will require two steps to find the final answer. This may mean writing two simple equations and solving the first to get a part needed for the second equation. We'll call these **complex problems.**

Many people have found the circle or pie representation of the formula an easy way to memorize the few formulas needed to solve most real estate problems. The pie tells us when to divide or multiply.

2 X ? = 6

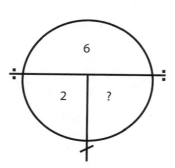

? X 2 = 6

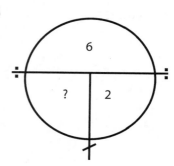

3 X 2 = ?

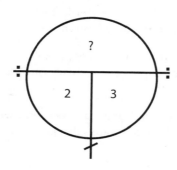

I. Percentage-Type Problems (Simple)

Percentage-type problems include commission problems, interest problems, appreciation, depreciation, profit/loss, and many more.

Whole x Percent = Part

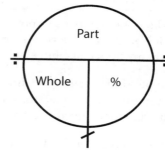

1. Fifty percent of a section is how many acres?

50% x 640 acres = ? acres or

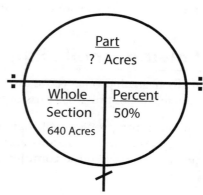

Answer: 320 Acres

2. Ten percent of an acre is how many square feet?

10% x 43,560 sq. ft. = ? sq. ft.

Part
? Sq. Ft.

Whole
1 sq. Acre
43,560

Percent
10%

Answer: 4,356.0 Sq. Ft.

3. Eighty acres is **what part of a section**?

$$? = \frac{80}{640} = \frac{1}{8} = 0.125 = 12.5\%$$

Part
80 Acres

Whole
640
Acres

Percent
?

Answer: 12.5%

4. If you calculated that your lot is 14,520 square feet, how many acres would you have?

One acre x percentage = part

43,560 sq. ft. x ? = 14,520

$$? = \frac{14,560}{43,560} = 0.3343 = 33.43 \text{ of an acre}$$

Part
14520

Whole
43,560

Percent
?

Answer: 33.43 of an acre

5 A. A nine and one-half percent interest rate on a $45,000 loan balance would require an annual interest payment of how much?

9.5% x $45,000 = Annual Interest Payment

?
Annual Interest

Loan
Balance
$45,000

Annual
Interest
Rate 9.5%

Answer: $4,275 annually

5 B. In the above example what would the monthly payment be?

$$\frac{\$4{,}275 \text{ yearly}}{12 \text{ Months}} \quad = \quad ? \quad = \$356.25 \text{ per month}$$

Answer: $356.25 monthly

6. The annual interest payment was $10,200 on a $120,000 loan. What was the annual interest rate?

Loan Balance x Annual Interest Rate = Annual Interest
  $120,000   x ?   = $10,200

Answer: $\dfrac{\$10{,}200}{\$120{,}000} = 8.5\%$

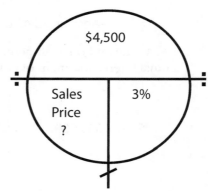

Part
$10,200

Whole
Loan
$12,000

Percent
Annually
?

7. Your commission is one-half of the 7% total commission on a $45,000 sale. How much do you get?

Sales Price x Commission Rate = Total Commission

$45,000 x 7% = Total Commission = $3,150

Total Commission ÷ 2 = Your commission = $1,575

Total
Commission ?

$45,000 | Commission
7%

8. If your 3% commission amounted to $4,500, how much did the property sell for?

Sale price x 3% = Commission = $4,500

Sales price = $\dfrac{\$4{,}500}{3\%}$

Answer: $150,000

$4,500

Sales
Price
?

3%

9. What was your commission rate (percentage) if you received $2,800 on a $56,000 sale?

Sales price x commission rate = commission

$56,000 x commission rate = $2,800

Answer: Commission Rate = $2,800/$56,000
= 0.05 or 5%

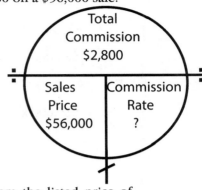

10. If your client is not willing to come down more than 10% from the listed price of $113,000, what is the minimum offer you would expect your client to accept?

$113,000 less 10% = Minimum Offer
or
$113,000 x 90% = Minimum Offer

Answer: $101,700

11. Your client says he wants to clear (net) $53,000 after commission. What must you sell the property for if you want a 7% commission?

100% of the selling price 7% of the selling price = Net to Owner

93% of selling price = $53,000

Selling Price = $53,000
93%

Owner

100% Selling Price
7% Commission
93% Net to

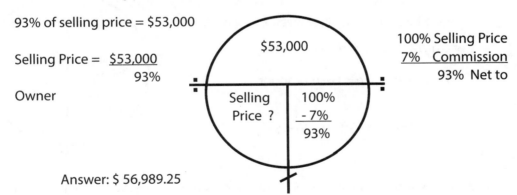

Answer: $ 56,989.25

12. A home that was purchased for $83,000, sold for $73,000. What was the percent of loss or depreciation?

$83,000 cost – $73,000 sales price = $10,000 loss

$10,000 is ?% of the cost?

$10,000 = ?% x $83,000

$$? = \frac{\$10,000}{\$83,000}$$

Answer: % loss = 12.05%

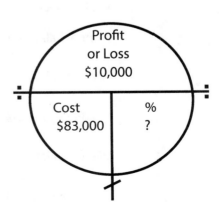

13. A home has appreciated by 13%. If it cost $89,000, how much is it worth now?

Original cost plus appreciation = current value

$89,000+13% of original cost = current value

or

$89,000 x 113% = current value

Answer: $100,570

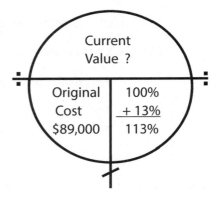

14. A bank will loan you 80% of the purchase price of a property, but will not loan you more than $58,500. How much could you pay for the property?

80% x cost of property = $58,500

Cost of Property = $\dfrac{\$58,500}{80\%}$

Answer: $73,125

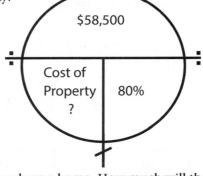

15. A bank will loan you 3 times your yearly income to purchase a home. How much will the bank loan you if your weekly pay is $375?

Yearly Income = $375 per week x 52 weeks

Yearly Income = $375 x 52 = $19,500

3 x Yearly Income = Loan Amount

Answer: 3 x $19,500 = $58,500

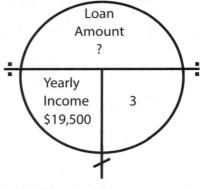

16. A bank is willing to loan you 3.3 times your annual salary. What would your minimum weekly salary need to be to justify a $90,000 loan?

Annual Salary x 3.3 = $90,000

Annual Salary = $\dfrac{\$90,000}{3.3}$ = $27,272.73

Weekly Salary = Annual Salary ÷ 52

Weekly Salary = $\dfrac{\$27,272.73}{52}$ = $524.48

Answer: $524.48

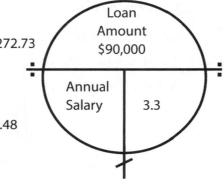

17. A property listed for $50,000 is appraised for $52,000. The loan to value ratio established by the bank is 85%. How much will the bank loan you?

The bank will make loans based on appraised value or market value, whichever of the two is lower. The listed price is irrelevant.

Appraised Value x Loan Percentage = Loan

$52,000 x 85% = Loan

Answer: $44,200

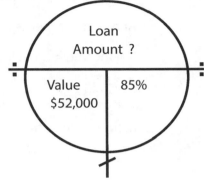

18. If a bank will lend you $60,000 on a loan to value ratio of 75%, what is the appraised value of the property you wish to buy?

Loan Percentage = Loan Amount/Appraised value

Appraised Value x Loan Percentage = Loan Amount

Appraised Value x 75% = $60,000

$$\text{Appraised Value} = \frac{\$60,000}{75\%}$$

Answer: $80,000

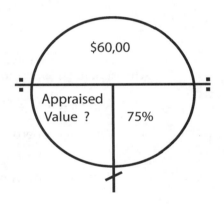

19 A. You purchased a piece of property for $40,000 and resell it for $60,000. What is your percentage of profit?

$$\text{Percentage Profit} = \frac{\text{What you made}}{\text{What you paid}} = \frac{\$20,000}{\$40,000} = 50\%$$

Profit was $60,000 sales price minus $40,000 purchase price = $20,000 (what you made)

19 B. What was your annual rate of return if you held the property five years?

The total % of gain divided by the number of years gives us an annualized rate of return.

Annual rate of return = 50% ÷ 5 years = 10% per year

(This is an example of straight-line appreciation)

20. A condominium appraised at $63,000 rents for $500 monthly. The maintenance fee of $80 a month is paid by the owner. The tenant pays $110 monthly utilities. What is the owner's annual rate of return for this property?

Annualized income is $500 monthly x 12 months = $6,000

Annualized expenses are $80 monthly x 12 months = $960

Net income = Gross Income minus Expenses = $5,040

Note: Since the tenant pays the utilities, these expenses are not subtracted from the owner's gross income. Annual rate of return =8.45% State uses an average value on rate of return; it is not compounded.

Return on Investment $= \dfrac{\text{Net Income}}{\text{Money Invested}}$

$$= \dfrac{\$5,040}{\$63,000} = 8\%$$

Answer: 8%

21. If an investor wants a 9% return on an income property producing $1,825 net monthly, what should he expect to pay for the property?

Annual return = $1,825 monthly x 12 months = $21,900/year

Value of property x rate of return = Net annual income

Value of property $= \dfrac{\text{Net Annual Income}}{\text{Rate of Return}} = \dfrac{\$21,900}{9\%}$

Answer: $243,333.33

J. Ratio Problems

Ratios compare portions of a whole. Simple fraction problems easily convert to percentages using ratios. If you play the horses, you see ratios of 3 to 2, 5 to 3, 2 to 1, etc. Let's look at some examples:

"3 to 2" – Should be interpreted as one part is 3/5 of the total (60%) and the other is 2/5(40%) of the total. The total is 3 + 2 or 5. Another way of looking at the ratio is 3/2. This says that 3 is 1.5 times greater than two. (3 ÷ 2 = 1.5) If we look at the ratio of 60% to 40%, it's obvious that 60% is 1.5 times greater than 40%.

K. Commission Problems

1. Commissions can be split many ways. Many times there are two brokers involved—the listing broker and selling broker—who share the total commission. The commission is also split between the broker and his salespeople. Finally, the third and fourth levels of commission split can be by a sales agent and her broker, who refers a listing or buyer to the listing or selling broker.

2. Typical flow of commission is as follows:

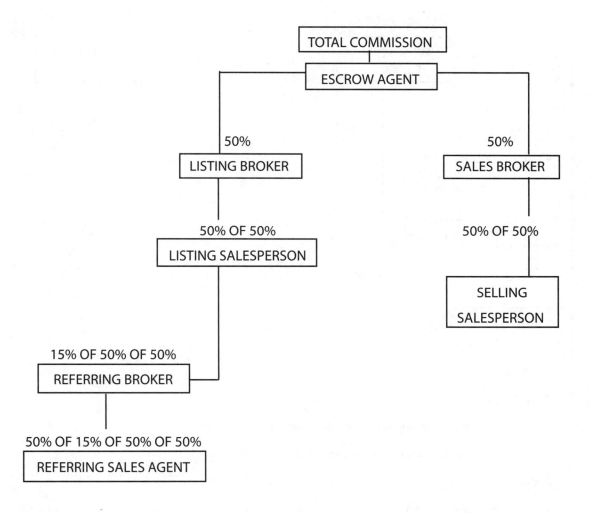

EXAMPLE:

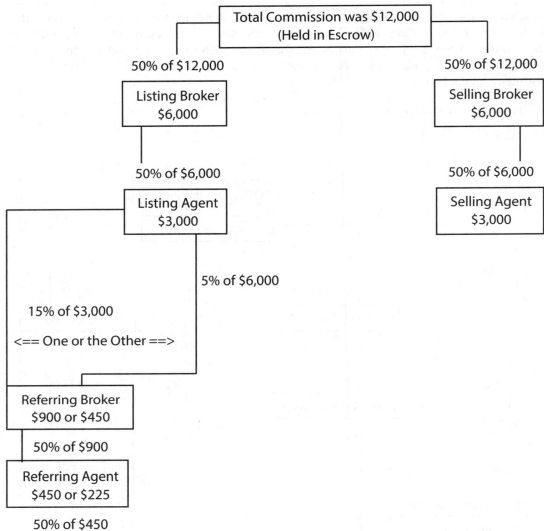

Trick Questions:

a) How much net income does the listing broker receive?

b) How much does the referring agent receive?

ANSWERS:

a) List broker grossed $6,000 but his net was $3,000 after paying his listing agent, and only $2,100 if he paid the referral broker.

b) Depends on whether he gets 15% of broker's commission, 15% of agent's commission, 15% of $6,000 or 15% of $3,000 (must be specified).

3. Commissions are a percentage of the total sale price. The basic formula is:

Commission Rate x Sales Price = Commission

% Commission x Sales Price = Commission

As with all formulas, we must be given two out of the three parts. Examples are as follows:

a) Mr. Prim, a real estate person, sold a house for $96,000 and the listing contract called for a 6.5% commission to the broker. What was the total commission?

% Commission x Sales Price = Commission

6.5% x $96,000 = Commission = $6,240

b) If the commission on a $169,000 sale was $11,830, what was the commission rate?

Commission Rate x Sales Price = Commission

$$\text{Commission Rate} = \frac{\text{Commission}}{\text{Sales Price}} = \frac{\$11,830}{\$169,000} = 7\%$$

c) Mr. Prim's broker received $7,200 as the listing broker's share of a commission. If Mr. Prim's agreement with his broker is to receive 40% of the earned commission, what would Mr. Prim's commission be?

40% x $7,200 = Mr. Prim's Commission = $2,880

d) (1) Mr. Prim received a lead from his broker, which was referred by an agent of another brokerage company. When Mr. Prim sold the property, it was agreed that Mr. Prim would have one-half of the referral fee deducted from his share of the commission. If the broker agreed to pay the referral brokerage 15%, how much commission was held back from Mr. Prim to be paid to the referring brokerage company? (Assume that Mr. Prim's broker received 55% of the total $5,500 commission)

(Referral %) times (Prim's broker commission) equals (Referral Fee)

15%	x	(55% x $5,500)	=	Referral fee
15%	x	($3,025)	=	Referral fee
			=	$453.75

Mr. Prim's portion (held back) = 50% of $453.75 = $226.88

d) (2) How much commission did the referring sales agent receive if he had a 50% agreement with his broker?

50% of referral fee = referral agents commission
50% of $453.75 = referral agents commission = $226.88

e) A referring sales agent received $510 commission from his broker after the sale of a property. The referral was to the listing broker who received 50% of the total commission and paid a 20% referral fee. If the referring sales agent received 50% of the referral fee, how much did the property sell for if the commission rate specified on the listing agreement was 6%?

Answer: First, write down our simple commission formula

Commission Rate (%) times Sales Price = Total Commission

6% x Sales Price = Total Commission

Second, we notice that we do not yet know two out of the three parts of the formula. Therefore we have to calculate the total commission backwards based on the $510 we know at the bottom of the commission chain.

Referring broker's commission times 50% equals referring sales agent commission.

Referring broker's commission x 50%	= $510	
Referring broker's commission	= $510 / 50%	= $1,020

Listing broker's share of commission times 20% equals referring broker's commission.

Listing broker's commission x 20%	= $1,020	
Listing broker's commission	= $1,020 / 20%	= $5,100

Total commission times 50% equals listing broker's commission

$$\text{Total commission} = \frac{\$5,100}{50\%} = \$10,200$$

Commission rate (%) times sales price equals total commission

% x Sales Price	= $10,200	
Sales Price = $10,200 / 6%	= $170,000	

4. Commission and sales prices are sometimes disguised and the problem needs to be expressed only in terms of percentages.

(Sales price) less (Commission) equals gross to owner

(Sales price) times (Commission rate) equals commission

Sales price less (sales price times commission rate) equals gross to owner. Notice we replaced "commission rate" with an equivalent term in the ( ).

Example: If there is a commission to be paid of 6.5% how much does an owner net after a sale?

REMEMBER: (% Commission) times (Sales Price) is Commission

(100% of sales price) less (6.5% of sales price) = Net to Owner

(100% 6.5%) of sales price   = net to owner

93.5% of sales price   = net to owner

sales price   = net to owner
          93.5%

If an owner wants to net $100,000 after paying a 6% commission what must he sell his property for?

100% of Sales Price 6% of Sales Price   = $100,000

94% of Sales Price   = $100,000

Sales Price   = $100,000 = $106,382.97
          94%

L. Complex Percentage Problems (More Than One Step!)

1. Complex Word Problem

Example: Three quarters of a section of land is worth ten thousand dollars. How much would 320 acres cost?

Step 1: What does one acre cost?

Price per acre x number of acres = purchase price

Price per acre x (3/4 of 640) = $10,000

Price per acre x (0.75 of 640) = $10,000

Price per acre x 480 = $10,000

Price per acre = $10,000 = $20.83
          480

Step 2:

Answer: Price of 320 acres = $20.83 x 320 = $6,665.60

2. If 50 is 20% of a number, what percent of that number would 75 be?

50 = 20% x a number

Step 1:

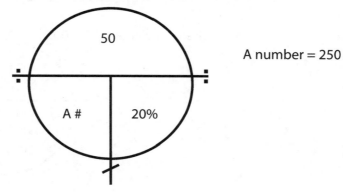

A number = 250

Step 2:   A number x ?% = 75

250 x ?% = 75

Answer: ?% = 75/250 = 30%

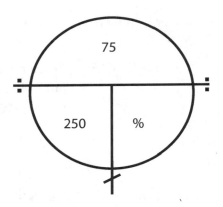

3. Salesperson Al sells a property listed by broker Bee. The property sold for $50,000 and the commission rate was 7% of the total sales price. How much commission did sales person Al receive if he receives 40% of his broker's share of the commission? (Assume listing and selling brokers split the commission equally.)

Total commission = 7% x $50,000 = $3,500
Al's broker receives 50% x $3,500 or $1,750
Al's share is 40% of $41,750 or $700

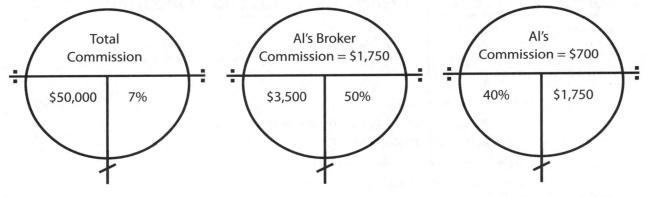

4. A $75,000 note is amortized over 10 years. The simple interest rate is 8.75%. What is the next monthly payment (principal and interest) if the note has a balance of $56,250?

Step 1:   We know how to calculate interest.
Loan balance x interest rate = Annual Interest
$56,250 x 8.75% = $4,921.88
Monthly Interest = $4,921.88 ÷ 12 months

Next interest payment = $410.16

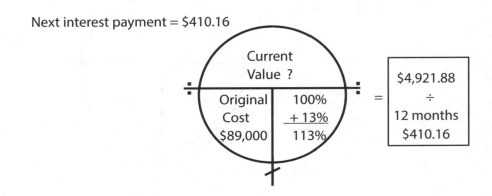

Step 2: We are told that the total principal is paid over 10 years (120 months) monthly payment x 120 months = $75,000

$$\text{Monthly payment} = \frac{\$75,000}{120 \text{ months}} = \$625 \text{ per month (Second step answer)}$$

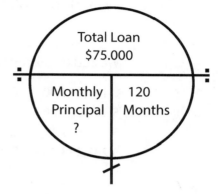

Total Loan
$75.000

Monthly Principal ? | 120 Months

Final Answer:

The question asks for the next monthly payment.

Payment = Principal + Interest
Payment = $625 + $410.16 = $1,035.16

5. The commission on a sale was $16,500. The listing contract specified 7% commission on the first $150,000, 5% on the next $100,000, and 3% on the balance. What was the sales price of the property?

Organization of the given data makes this problem easy. We will break this problem down into three simple commission problems:

Statement 1: $150,000 x 7% = $10,500

Statement 2: $100,000 x 5% = $5,000

Statement 3:   Balance of x 3% = Balance of $16,500
               Sales Price   Commission   − $15,500
                                                    $ 1,000

TOTALS $16,500   33,333

Only Statement 3 has unknown data to be determined.

Step 1: The question asks for **total sales price.** The question does give us the total commission so we can easily calculate that portion of the 3% commission in Statement 3 by subtracting statement 1 and 2 commissions from the total commission.

$16,500 total commission minus $10,500 minus $5,000 = $1,000

Step 2: What is the remainder of the sales price that received a 3% commission rate?

Remainder of sales price x 3% = $1,000

Remainder of sales price $\quad$ = $1,000 ÷ 3%

$\qquad$ = $33,333.33

We add up all portions to get a final answer.

$ 150,000.00	7% commission
$ 100,000.00	5% commission
$ 33,333.33	3% commission
$ 283,333.33	Total Sales Price

Answer: $283,333.33

6. A speculator wants to make <u>10% per annum profit</u> on his property after taking into account all expenses and sales commission of 7%. If his annual expenses were $825 and he paid $36,000 for the property 8 years ago, what must he sell the property for now?

Statement 1: Profit must be 10% per year x 8 years or 80%

Statement 2: Expenses were $825 per year x 8 years or $6,600

Statement 3: Commission is 7% of the selling price

Step 1: The total money to owner is original costs plus expenses plus profit or $36,000 + $6,600 + $28,800 = $71,400.

Step 2: Owner gets 100% of sales price less 7% of sales price or 93% of the selling price since commission is 7%

Sales price x 93% = Net to owner

Sales price x 93% = $71,400 $\qquad \dfrac{\$71,400}{93\%}$

Sales price = 93%

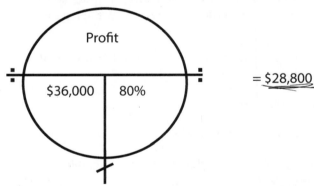

Answer: Property sells for $76,774.19

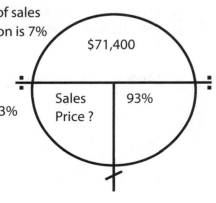

7. An agent has the choice of managing an apartment building for 3% of the gross income or 5% of the net income. There are 4 two-bedroom apartments that each rent for $395 monthly; 6 one-bedroom apartments that each rent for $295 monthly and 2 efficiencies that each rent for $195 monthly. There is typically a 10% vacancy rate and expenses include water at $100 monthly, electric at $900 monthly and general maintenance and grounds upkeep at $250 monthly.

Gross income is:

4 Apts. @ $395 month   = $1,580 month
6 Apts. @ $295 month   = $1,770 month
2 Effc. @ $195 month   = $ 390 month
                                $3,740 month potential gross income

Less 10% typical vacancy = $3,740 x 10% = $374.00
$3,740 $374 = $3,366.00 monthly effective gross income

Choice 1:   3% of monthly effective gross income = monthly commission
             3% x $3,366.00 = $101 monthly commission

Choice 2:   5% of net monthly income
             (Gross monthly income) less (Expenses) = Monthly net income
             $3,740 (gross income) $374.00 = $3,366.00
             $3,366.00 $1,250 (expenses) = $2,116.00 net income
             $2,116.00 x 5% = $105.80

Answer: Choice 2 pays more commission.

M. Taxes

Property has a pseudo official value called the appraised value. Many properties are rarely assessed except for the tax collector. The tax collector, for a specific area, has an assessment rate usually 35% of appraised value. To determine the assessed value, the final tax bill is computed by multiplying the assessed value times the tax rate. Taxes are always calculated on an annual basis.

Assessed Value   = (Appraised Value) x (Assessment Rate)

Tax Bill   = (Assessed Value) x (Tax Rate)

The tax rate can be given in dollars per $1,000 of assessed value (known as mills) or in dollars per $100 of assessed value.

Example: A home appraised for $50,000 has a local assessment rate of 50%. What is the assessed value of the home?

Assessed Value   = (Appraised Value) x (Assessment Rate)

$25,000   = $50,000   x   50%

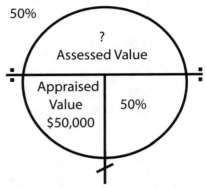

Answer: $25,000

Example: What would the tax bill be if the tax rate is $5.50 per $100 of assessed value and the assessed value is $25,000?

(Tax Rate) x (Assessed Value) = Tax Bill

$$\frac{\$5.50}{\$100} \; x \;\; \$25,000 \; = \; 0.055 \; x \; \$25,000 \; = \; \$1,375$$

(1) A property appraised for $62,000 is assessed at 40% of that value. If the tax rate is 9 mills, what is the tax bill?

(Appraised Value)   x (Assessed Rate) = Assessed Value

$62,000   x   40%   = $24,800

(Assessed Value)   x   (Tax Rate)   = Tax Bill

$$\$24,800 \;\;\;\;\;\; x \;\; \frac{9}{1,000} \;\; = \$24,800 \; x \; 0.009$$

Answer: $223.20

(2) The Assessment Rate in a particular township is 35%. Tax rates are: School 12 mills, Township 9 mills, County 3 mills and Special Levy 4 mills. If a property owner's total tax bill is $2,150 per year, what's the property's appraised value?

This problem is the same as all other tax problems except we will work it backwards.

Step 1:   Tax Bill = (Assessed Value) x (Tax Rate)
           (Since we know 2 of 3 parts of the equation, we're home free!)

$2,150   =   ?   x   (12 + 9 + 3 + 4 mills)

$$\frac{\$2,150}{28 \text{ mills}} = ?$$

$$\frac{\$2,150}{0.028} = \$76,785.71$$

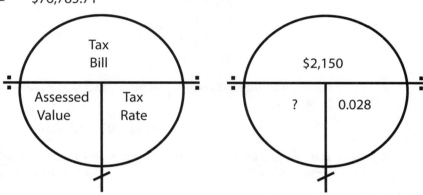

       Answer: $76,785.71

Step 2:   (Appraised Value) x (Assessment Rate) = Assessed Value
           {Again, we know 2 of the 3 parts of the equation}

(Appraised Value) x35%   = $76,785.71

$$\text{Appraised Value} = \frac{\$76,785.71}{35\%} = \$219,387.74$$

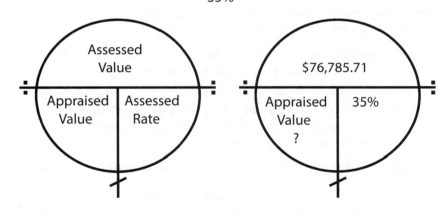

       Answer: $219,387.74

N. Conveyance or Transfer Fees *

The conveyance or transfer fee (seller expense) is paid by the seller at closing. It is based on the selling price of the property. The formula is 10 cents per $100 or 1 mill (.001) of the selling price and fraction thereof. The transfer fee can be understood by looking at examples and working different problems.

Selling Price	Transfer Fee
53,300.00	53.30
53,300.09	53.40
53,111.11	53.20
53,400.00	53.40
53,400.01	53.50

One of the simplest ways to calculate the transfer fee is to multiply the selling price by 1 mill (0.001).

$$53,401.00 \times 0.001 = 53.40100$$

Transfer fee must end with "0." Examples include 0.10, 0.20, 0.30, 0.40, 0.50, 0.60, 0.70, 0.80, 0.90. Any extra numbers will add 0.10 or 10 cents to the existing number.

Step 1: 53.40100

Step 2: 53.4

Step 3: Does the transfer fee have all zeros to the right of the "4" in Step 1?

Answer: NO, there is a "1" in the "0100," so, add 0.10 to the 53.4 in Step 2.

$$\$53.4 + 0.10 = \$53.50 \qquad \$53.50 \text{ is the transfer fee}$$

Conveyance fee, transfer tax, auditors tax and state documentary stamps are synonymous terms.

O. Proration of Expenses or Income

Expenses or income, either prepaid or paid in arrears, are divided between buyer and seller at closing. Items are prorated over time.

Example: Monthly interest on a mortgage is $330 and is paid through the end of the month. If a seller closed on the sale on the 10th of the next month, how much interest would he owe?

Solution: The owner does not owe for the entire month since he paid off the loan on the 10th day. Therefore, all we have to do is calculate for what portion of a month he did owe the bank interest.

Assuming a 30-day month, then 10 days would be one-third of a month.

$$\text{Seller's Portion} = \frac{\text{Portion of Time Used}}{\text{Total Time Period}} \times \text{Amount of Prorate}$$

$$\frac{10 \text{ days}}{30 \text{ days}} = \frac{1}{3} \times \$330$$

$$0.3333 \times \$330 = \$109.989 = \$110$$

It makes sense that the seller must pay the expenses up to the closing date and is entitled to any credits for prepaid items up to the closing date. Therefore, we will always calculate the seller's portion. Problems involving taxes, insurance, and income property will involve a buyer. The buyer portion is what's left over after we calculate the seller's portion.

1) The annual taxes for 2014 are due January 1, 2015. They are $314 semi-annually. The property closed June 15, 2014. How much will the seller owe at closing for taxes?

Total taxes for the year are $314 semi-annually x 2 = $628 yearly

Seller's Portion = (Portion of Time Used) x (Amount to Prorate)

$$\frac{5.5 \text{ Months}}{12 \text{ Months}} \quad x \quad \$628 \text{ yearly}$$

0.458 x $628 = $287.63

Remember: Close counts on the exam, so choose the closest answer using the above method, or one of the following

Alternate Solution:

Draw a timeline

Count the months and stop the month before closing, then how much into June, half a month (count on your fingers to be sure).

Calculate the tax for one month:

$628 ÷ 12 months = $52.33 per month

Seller's Portion = 5.5 months x $52.33 = $287.82

Most exact calculation: (They will give you a calendar to use exact days.)

$628 ÷ 365 days   = $1.7205/day

Seller's Portion =   166 days used x $1.7205/day
          = $285.61

Answer: $285.61

| Jan-31 days |
| Feb-28 days |
| Mar-31 days |
| Apr-30 days |
| May-31 days |
| Jun-15 days=166 |

2)   The insurance premium was paid July 1, 2013 for a 3-year period. The total premium was $1,128. If the buyer assumed the policy on the date of closing, January 20, 1988, what is the seller's credit?

The seller's credit is the portion he already paid for but he didn't live there. In other words, the seller's credit is the buyer's portion or the time the buyer will live there.

$1,128 3/yr. ÷ 3 years = $ 376/year

$376 ÷ 365 days = $1.0301 per day

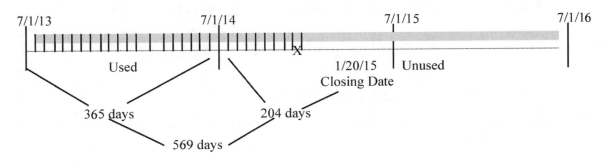

$1.0301 per day   x   569 days = $586.13

$1,128 3/years - $586.13 used = $541.87 Seller's Credit

3. Rent of $350 has been paid to the seller for the month of August. The property had been sold and closing was August 11th. What will the buyer's credit for rent be?

$350/month ÷ 30 days = $11.6667 per day

30 days 11 days = 19 days

$11.6667/day x 19 days = $221.6667 = $221.67 Buyer's Credit

Answer: $221.67

II. Problem Solving

A. The "Magic" Pie or Circle Equation

The first "formula" (aid) we are going to learn is the circle, or pie, equation. The pie can be used for a large portion of the problems and is an aid to tell you when to divide or multiply. Some of the problem types include interest, rate of return on an income property, percentage of appreciation or depreciation, and many more.

1. The Basics

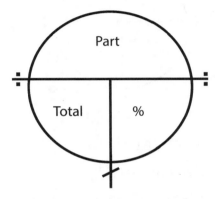

The circle equation is made up of the part, the total, and the percent. What the pie tells us is:

    a.   Part equates total times percent
               part = total x %

    b.   Total equals part divided by percent
               total = part ÷ %

    c.   Percent equals part divided by total
               % = part ÷ total

The part is usually the smallest number in a problem, but not always. Usually, we are dealing with percentages smaller than 100%. If the percentage is greater than 100%, then the part is larger than the total, as we will explain later. The part can be obtained by multiplying % times total.

The total is usually the largest number, with the same exceptions as the part defined above. The total can be calculated by dividing the part by %.

The % can be calculated by dividing the part by the total. In most problems, it is less than 100%, but not always as we'll see in appreciation problems.

The % box can also be in the form of a fraction or decimal. Maybe we should say if the problem is in the form of a fraction or decimal, you can convert that to percent.

Breaking Problems Down For The Pie

The challenge of each problem is to know when to multiply and when to divide. These are the only possible steps to solving problems other than adding and subtracting. There are only three slots in the pie and the problem must give us two of the three numbers.

Key word — "OF" (means multiply)

Example 1: One-half of a dollar is how much?

	%	x	Total	=	Part
or	_	x	$1.00	=	Part
or	0.5	x	$1.00	=	Part
or	50%	x	$1.00	=	Part

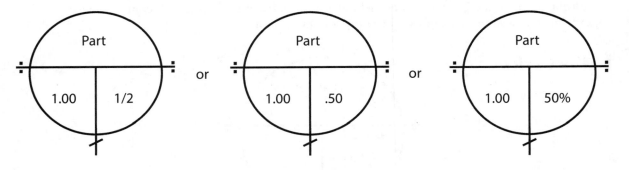

Convert fractions to decimal equivalents.

1/2 is (1 ÷ 2) and equals 0.5

3 1/2 is 3 + (1 ÷ 2) and equals 3.5

Convert decimals to percentages.

Move the decimal point two places to the right (multiply by 100).

Example 2: $400 is 2 1/2% of what amount? $400 ÷ 2.5% = $16,000

0.5	is 5.0%	fifty percent
0.505	is 50.5%	fifty and a half percent
3.5	is 350.0%	three hundred and fifty percent

Note: You can add zeros to the end of decimal numbers without changing its value

Example 3: A commission on a $35,000 home sale was $2,200. What was the commission rate?

(a)   We want to know commission which is a %

(b)   Therefore, the problem must give us the total and the part.

(c)   The commission ($2,200) is obviously only a part of the selling price ($35,000)

(d)
$$\% = \frac{Part}{Total}$$ or   Part ÷ Total = Percentage

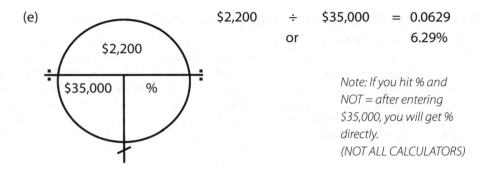

(e)

$2,200   ÷ $35,000   =   0.0629
or   6.29%

Note: If you hit % and NOT = after entering $35,000, you will get % directly.
(NOT ALL CALCULATORS)

2. Complex Problems (More Than One Calculation)

Sometimes the problem will require two calculations to get the answer. Relax, read the question, and write down the givens. Two out of three pieces of the secondary pie will be given—solve to get the second of the three parts needed for the primary pie.

Mr. Smith gets two-thirds of the seven percent commission on a $79,000 home sale. How much was Mr. Smith's commission?

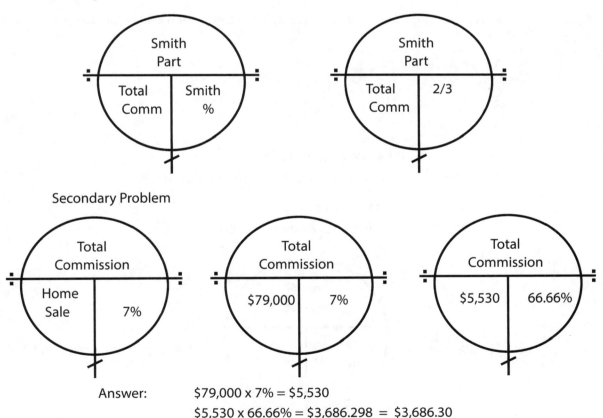

Primary Problem

Secondary Problem

Answer: $79,000 x 7% = $5,530
             $5,530 x 66.66% = $3,686.298 = $3,686.30

3. Interest Problems – Amortized and Term Loans

There are two (2) types of loans we need to understand, amortized loans and term loans. First, let's cover amortized loans. An amortized loan is our typical home mortgage loan where the payment stays the same over the life of the loan, but the principal in each payment varies. We are not bankers and do not need to calculate principal. We do need to compute interest and, once we learn how easy it is, we can subtract the interest from the total payment to determine how much of the payment is being applied to the principal (or tell us what the principal is). Let's do some basic interest problems!

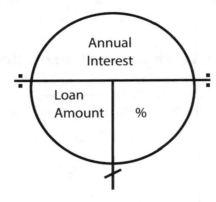

(a)   What is the annual interest rate on a $73,000 loan with monthly interest payments of $821.25?

    1.   11.25%

    2.   13.5%

    3.   15.0%

    4.   10.5%

First:	What are we looking for?
Answer:	% (we can also see that all the answers are %.)
Second:	What formula can I use?
Answer:	The circle—it's an interest problem.

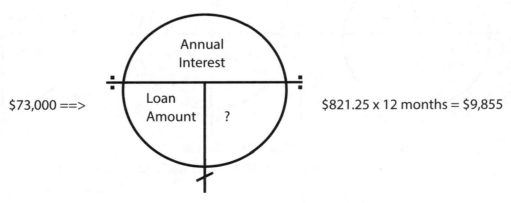

Remember: The "PART" must always be an "ANNUAL AMOUNT." That is why we multiplied the monthly interest by 12.

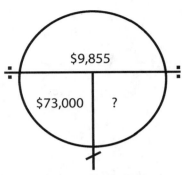

Now, put it into your calculator just how you read it—$9,855 ÷ $73,000 = 0.135—OOPS! But all the answers are in %. Remember: Convert a decimal to a %, just multiply by 100, or move the decimal 2 places to the right.

Answer: #2 (13.5%)

(b) A quarterly interest expense of $650 represents an 11% rate on what amount?

1. $5,909.10
2. $70,909.09
3. $11,818.20
4. $23,636.36

First: What are we looking for?

Answer: The loan amount (THE TOTAL)

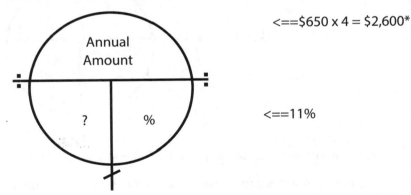

Remember: The "PART" must always be annual amount. That is why we multiplied the quarterly interest payments by 4.

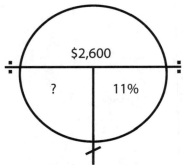

Now, put it into your calculator just how you read it: 2,600 ÷ 11% is $23,636.36.

Remember: To enter % for 11%. Do not hit the = sign. After you hit %, the # on your calculator is the answer. (NOT ALL CALCULATORS)

Answer: #4 ($23,636.36)

(c)   What is the monthly interest on a mortgage of **$54,600** at annual interest rate of **13.25%?**

    1. $ 723.40

    2. $ 602.88

    3. $7,234.50

    4. $ 816.00

First: **What are we looking for?**

Answer: **Monthly interest (the "PART" ÷ 12 months)**

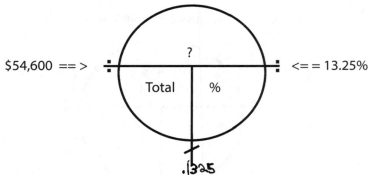

Now, put it into your calculator like this: **$54,600 x 13.25% is $7,234.50***

Again, you do not need to hit the = key. After you press %, the number on your calculator is the answer for that step.

*Remember: The "PART" is an annual amount. You must divide by 12 to get monthly interest.

$7,234.50 ÷ 12 mos. = $602.88/month

$54,600 x 13.25% is $7,234.50*

Answer: #2 ($602.88)

(d) If 12% is the annual rate of interest and the monthly interest payment is $360, what is the amount of the loan?

1.　$36,000
2.　$ 3,600
3.　$ 3,000
4.　$ 4,320

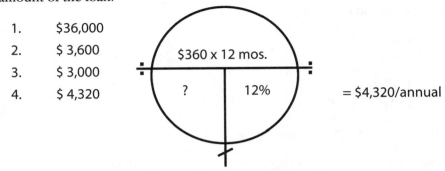

= $4,320/annual

Answer: #1 ($36,000)

Note: Most payments are made of principal and interest. Principal is that portion of a payment that reduces the total balance owed on the loan. We don't know how to compute this amount nor do we need to know. We do know how to calculate the monthly interest and subtract the monthly interest from the total payment. The difference, or what's left, is the amount of the payment going toward the principal.

(e) Monthly payments on a mortgage are $1,025, including principal and interest. If the payoff on the mortgage is $93,000 and the annual interest rate is 10.5%, what is the principal amount of the next payment?

1.　$　813.75
2.　$　211.25
3.　$　107.63
4.　$1,236.25

Remember the first step:　　What am I looking for?

Answer:　　　　　　　　　Next monthly principal

Remember: Just because a question is long, doesn't mean it's difficult.

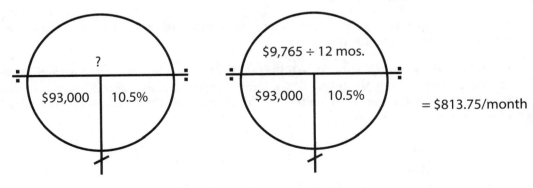

= $813.75/month

$93,000 x 10.5% = $9,765 (the "PART" or annual interest)

$9,765 ÷ 12 months = $813.75 monthly interest

Answer: #2, ($1,025 Total Payment $813.75 Interest = $211.25 Principal)

(f) There is a balance of $47,500 due on a contract which requires a monthly payment of $440 plus interest at a rate of 12% per annum. What is the amount of the next payment, including principal and interest?

    1. $ 440

    2. $ 475

    3. $1,355

    4. $ 915

First: What am I looking for?

Answer: Monthly payment of principal and interest

Remember: We don't know how to calculate principal. They have given us that amount. We do know how to compute interest.

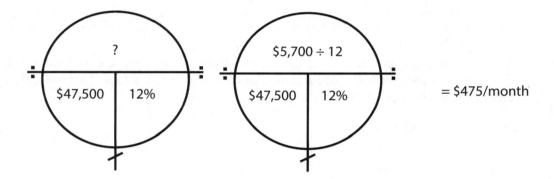

$47,500 x 12% = $5,700 (the "PART" or annual interest)

$5,700 ÷ 12 months = $475 monthly interest + $440 principal = $915 (Total Principal and Interest)

        Answer: #4 ($915)

Now we will approach what appear to be more difficult interest problems. These are also very simple once you know how.

(g) John and Kathy Smith obtain an $80,000 loan to buy a house. The mortgage payments are $822.89 per month, including 12% interest per year, payable over 30 years. How much total interest will they pay in the fifth year of the loan if principal reduction that year is 3.7% of the original loan amount?

    1. $6,640

    2. $6,915

    3. $9,600

    4. $9,875

First: What am I looking for?

Answer: The amount of interest paid in the 5th year.

We approach this as we did for a total monthly payment, only now we are looking at one year. What is the total mortgage payment? $822.89 per month, over 1 year how much is paid in total?

$822.89 x 12 months = $9,874.68 including principal and interest

The problem tells us that the amount paid to principal that year is 3.7 % of the original loan amount. How much is that?

$80,000 (loan amount) x 3.7%   = $2,960.00 principal

Total amount paid   = $9,874.68 principal and interest
(Less) $2,960.00 principal
$6,914.68 interest
(rounded up to the nearest answer #2)

Remember: The problem has to tell us how much was applied to the principal.

Answer: #2 ($6,915)

(h) Jamie Newell borrows $93,500 for a mortgage loan at 10.25%. The total monthly payment including principal and interest is $1,050. How much total interest did Jamie pay in the 8th year of the loan if principal reduction that year was 2.9% of the original loan amount?

1. $ 2,711.50
2. $ 3,654.00
3. $ 9,888.50
4. $12,600.00

paid to princ. 2,711.5

Answer: #3 ($9,888.50)

Here is another type of question you should be familiar with:

(i) Walt Fisher and his wife Betty, obtain a 30-year, $78,000 loan to buy a house. If loan payments are $698.98 per month, including 10 1/4% interest per year, and the second monthly payment includes $665.97 in interest, what will be the amount of interest paid over the life of the loan?

1. $125,813
2. $173,850
3. $239,850
4. $251,626

Believe it or not, this is in essence the same type of problem as the previous ones. Instead of one month's total interest payment, or the total interest paid in one year, this problem asks us for the total interest over 30 years. Let's approach it the same way as the others.

The total monthly payment including principal and interest is $698.98. How many total payments are we going to make over the life of the loan?

(30-year mortgage) x (12 months per year) = 360 total monthly payments
$698.98 x 360 months = $251,632.80 total paid over the life of the loan including principal and interest.

How much of that is principal over the life of the loan? That's right! The amount of the mortgage is $78,000.

$251,632.80   total principal and interest
Less - $ 78,000.00   loan amount
$173,632.80   interest

Answer: #2 ($173,626 the closest)

(j) A house sold for 15% less than its listing price of $134,900. The buyers borrowed $95,000 at 10.75% interest on a 20-year note. If the monthly mortgage payments are $921.08, how much interest will the buyers pay over the life of the loan?

1. $ 86,159.20
2. $ 12,606.00
3. $221,059.20
4. $126,059.20

240

Answer: #4 ($126,059.20)

(k) A home was purchased for $65,000. The loan amount was 80% of the purchase price on a 30-year note at 9 1/4% interest. The monthly payment including principal and interest was $8.14 per $1,000 of the loan on a 30-year mortgage. What was the total interest paid over the life of the loan?

1. $100,381
2. $152,380
3. $125,476
4. $221,650

Answer: #1 ($100,381 the closest)

Now let's cover straight-line amortized loans.

A straight-line amortized loan is a loan whose principal remains constant over the life of the loan and the amount of interest varies with each payment, such as a car loan. If one borrows $15,000 over 5 years and makes monthly payments, there will be 60 monthly payments of $250 each to repay the principal—plus interest. Let's say the interest rate is 12% per year. Each month the payment of principal, $250, remains constant, and the interest will vary based on the remaining balance.

Let's look at an example:

(l) Mary and Bob Johnson borrow $30,000 to build an addition to their home. The loan is for 4 years at 11% interest. If the principal is $625 per month, how much will Mary and Bob's 3rd payment be?

First: How many payments have Mary and Bob already made? 2, that's right. The amount they borrowed was reduced by $625 per month for 2 months.

$625 x 2 = $1,250 (already paid back)

They originally borrowed	$30,000
Less 2 payments already made	- $ 1,250
Before making the 3rd payment they owe	$28,750 plus interest at 11%.

$28,750 x 11% = $3,162.50, annual interest ÷ 12 = $263.54 interest per month

$625 principal + $263.54 interest = $888.54 3rd payment

(m) Using the same information in "(l)" how much would the 13th payment be? Remember: How many payments have already been made?

$625 x 12=$7,500

Amount originally borrowed	$30,000
Less Amount	-$ 7,500
	$22,500

$22,500 x 11% = $2,475 annual interest ÷12 = $206.25 interest payment

$625 principal + $206.25 interest = $831.25 13th payment

(n) The Harrisons borrowed $14,000 to build a swimming pool at their home. They agreed to repay the loan on a 5-year note at 10.25% per year. The principal amount of each payment is $233.33 per month. How much will the Harrisons' 5th payment be?

1. $933.33
2. $111.12
3. $344.94
4. $233.33

Answer: #3 ($344.94)

4. Capitalization Problems – Rate of Return on Investment

Now let's try some capitalization problems. It's almost the same as interest but the circle looks like this:

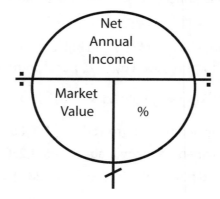

Remember: Net income is gross income minus expenses.

(a) An apartment building has a rate of return of 9%. The monthly net rental is $850. What is the market value of the property?

1. $94,444.44
2. $113,333.33
3. $102,000.00
4. $116,000.00

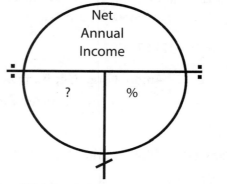

<==9

$850 x 12 months = $10,200 annual income

Note: This problem gives us monthly net income. We only have to make it an annual amount.

$850 x 12 months = $10,200/annual

$10,200 ÷ 9% =$113,333.33

Answer: #2 ($113,333.33)

(b)   An office building has a gross annual income of $64,000. Expenses are $3,230 per month. If the building is valued at $252,400, what is the owner's rate of return?

1.   25.36%
2.   10.00%
3.   15.36%
4.   24.07%

First: What are we looking for?

Answer: Rate of Return or %

Remember: The "PART" must always be net annual income. They give us gross annual income and monthly expenses so we must multiply monthly expenses by 12 months to get annual expenses. When we subtract the annual expenses from the gross annual income to get net annual income.

$3,230 x 12 months = $38,760 annual expenses

$64,000 (gross annual income) $38,760 = $25,240 net annual income

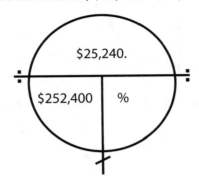

$25,240 net income ÷ $252,400 market value = 0.10 or 10%

Answer: #2 (10.00%)

(c) If a quarterly income of $1,250 yields an investor a 14% return, how much was paid for the property?

1. $ 8,928.57
2. $ 89,285.70
3. $ 35,714.29
4. $107,142.86

First: What are we looking for?

Answer: Value of the property/total

Remember: Quarterly income must be made into annual income.

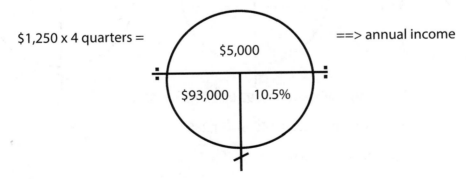

$5,000 ÷ 14% = $35,714.29 value

Answer: #3 ($35,714.29)

5. Commission Problems

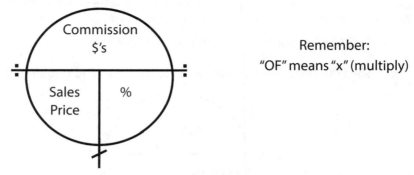

Remember:
"OF" means "x" (multiply)

(a) The commission on the sale of a $102,000 house is 6%. How much is the commission?

1. $170,000
2. $ 17,000
3. $ 612
4. $ 6,120

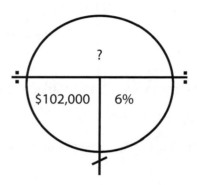

$102,000 sales price x 6% rate of commission = $6,120 total commission

Answer: #4 ($6,120)

(b) Your broker has agreed to pay you 40% of the company's share of the commission. The company received 3.5% of a $92,000 sale. What was your share of the commission?

1. $1,400
2. $1,288
3. $3,220
4. $3,680

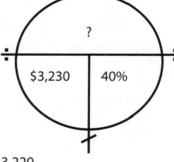

The company's portion: $92,000 x 3.5% = $3,220

Your portion: $ 3,220 x 40% = $1,288

Answer: #2 ($1,288)

(c) The agreed commission rate for selling an apartment building is 6% on the first $100,000 and 4% of anything over that amount. The total commission paid was $9,200. What was the sales price of the building?

1. $ 80,000
2. $100,000
3. $180,000
4. $150,000

This problem has several steps. Don't worry, each step is simple.

The total commission was $9,200. We know that 6% of $100,000 was part of it:

$100,000 x 6% = $6,000

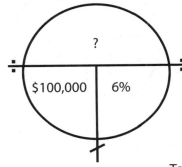

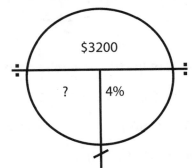

Total commission   = $9,200
minus $100,000 x 6%   = $6,000
Remainder of sales price x 4%   = $3,200

We also know that 4% of something = $3,200 or said another way, $3,200 is equal to 4% of?

Answer: $80,000 = =>

You're not done, though.

Remember: "What am I looking for?"—The sales price of the building! So, $100,000 + $80,000 = $180,000

Answer: #3 ($180,000)

(d) Sales associate Laura refers a listing on a $75,000 home and is to receive 15% of the total 7% commission if the property sells. Licensee Sam sells the property and Laura's 15% is deducted from Sam's 1/2 of the commission, how much will Sam receive?

1. $ 5,250.00
2. $ 787.50
3. $ 4,462.50
4. $ 1,837.50

Again, there are several steps to this problem. They're all easy, just take them one at a time. First, let's figure out the total commission.

The sales price was $75,000. The total commission was 7%.

$75,000 x 7% = $5,250 or

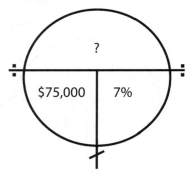

Laura is to receive 15% of $5,250 or $787.50

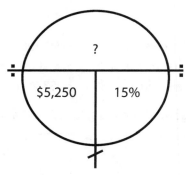

Sam receives 1/2 of the total commission minus Laura's portion.

Total commission $5,250 ÷ 2 = $2,625 (1/2 total commission)

$2,625 $787.50 (Laura's portion) = $1,837.50 Sam's commission

Answer: #4 ($1,837.50)

(e) Broker Susan Harris of ABC Realty recently listed and sold Jack and Jill Smith's home for $43,500. Harris charged the Smith's a 6 1/2% commission and will pay 55% of that amount to the listing person and selling salesperson, on a ratio of 6 to 5, respectively. What amount of commission will the listing salesperson receive from the Smiths' sale?

1. $1,555.13
2. $1,272.38
3. $ 848.25
4. $ 706.88

First we must figure the total commission.

(Sales Price)	x	(Commission Rate)	=	Total Commission
$43,500	x	6.5%	=	$2,827.50

A portion of the commission is to be shared by two (2) salespeople which in this case is 55%.

Total Commission $2,827.50
                                                  x   55%
Salespeople's portion of the commission $1,555.13

Listing person gets 6 parts out of a total 11 parts (6 to 5 ratio totals 11 parts).

Salesperson gets 5 parts of total 11 parts. The listing person gets 6/11 of $1,555.13.

$$\frac{6}{11} = 54.55\%$$

54.55% of salespeople portion of commission $1,555.13

$1,555.13 x 54.55% = $848.32

Answer: #3 ($848.25 is closest)

6. Appreciation and Depreciation

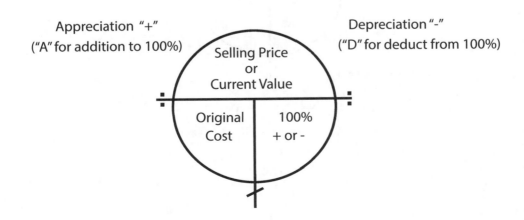

Appreciation "+"
("A" for addition to 100%)

Depreciation "-"
("D" for deduct from 100%)

Selling Price
or
Current Value

Original Cost

100%
+ or -

(a) If a building sold for $158,162 at a loss of 8%, what was the original cost of the building?

1. $145,509.04
2. $171,915.22
3. $170,814.96
4. $165,905.40

First: What are we looking for?
              Right! Original Cost

Now, is it a depreciation or an appreciation problem? Did the building lose money? Yes, so it's a depreciation problem.

Next, we always start with 100%. If it's a depreciation problem, we subtract how much it depreciated from 100%. If it appreciates, we add to 100% how much it appreciated. Think of "A" for appreciate and "A" for add; "D" for depreciation and "D" for deduct. This problem says the building depreciated 8%, so...

           100%
          – 8%
           92%

The selling price was $158,162. So...

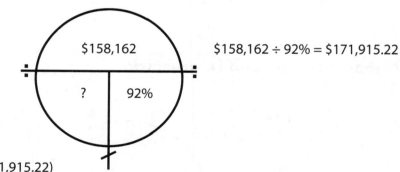

$158,162 ÷ 92% = $171,915.22

Answer : #2 ($171,915.22)

(b) A property has depreciated annually 2 1/2% for 7 years. The current depreciated value of the property is $95,000. What was the original cost? (Use straight-line depreciation basis).

1. $166,250.00
2. $ 94,833.75
3. $ 78,375.00
4. $115,151.52

This question is meant to throw you off by saying "use straight-line depreciation basis." That's the only kind we use! There is one extra step to this problem. We must calculate the total amount of depreciation. That's easy: 7 years x 2 1/2% = 17 1/2% Now the problem is just like the previous one.

First: What are we looking for?

Original cost.   And it's a depreciation problem so, we know that we *subtract* from
100%.

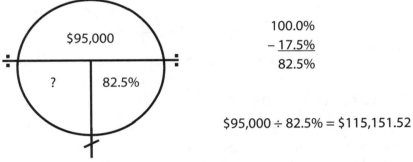

100.0%
− 17.5%
82.5%

$95,000 ÷ 82.5% = $115,151.52

Remember: Be careful to read your calculator correctly and select the correct answer.

Answer: #4 ($115,151.52)

(c) A house depreciated and is now worth $48,500, which is 82% of its original cost. What was the original cost of the property?

1. $39,770.00
2. $57,230.00
3. $59,146.34
4. $52,510.25

Again, it's the same kind of problem. We are looking for original cost. In this problem, we are already told what the house has depreciated to (we don't have to subtract from 100%).

$48,500 : 82% = $59,146.34

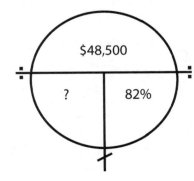

Answer: #3 ($59,146.34)

(d) A property that originally cost $93,500 has appreciated 25%. What is the property now worth?

1. $116,875.00
2. $ 70,125.00
3. $ 95,873.50
4. $110,250.25

This is an appreciation problem, so we'll add to 100% how much it appreciated.

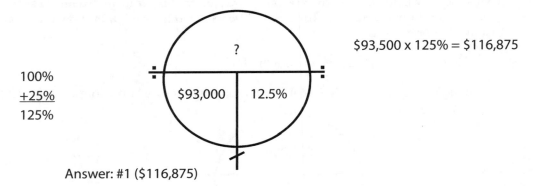

100%
+25%
125%

$93,500 x 125% = $116,875

Answer: #1 ($116,875)

7. Loan/Value Ratio

NOTE: Loan/value ratio is the % of the appraised value of the property that the bank will loan for a mortgage is the loan amount.

(a) If the loan/value ratio is 80/20, and the house is appraised for $75,000 how much will the buyer be permitted to borrower?

1. $45,000
2. $15,000
3. $75,000
4. $60,000

$75,000 x 80% = $60,000 loan amount
$75,000 x 20% = $15,000 equity or down payment

Answer: #4 ($60,000)

(b) Your client has been told he has been approved to obtain financing for a new home valued at 2 1/2 times annual salary. If the home she wants to buy is priced at $72,000, what must your client's monthly salary be?

1. $28,800
2. $ 2,400
3. $24,000
4. $ 240

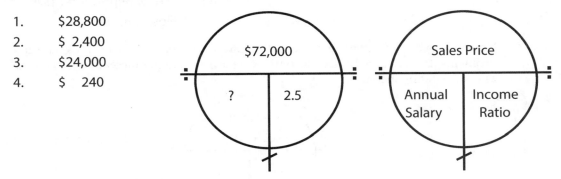

$72,000 (sales price) ÷ 2.5 = $28,800 (annual salary)

Remember, the question asks for monthly salary.

So, $28,800 ÷ 12 months = $2,400 per month.

Answer: #2 ($2,400)

8. Cash Flow On Income-Producing Property

It is important that we understand a basic cash flow statement for an income property—let's use a 10-unit apartment building—has a **potential gross income**. The potential gross income is the total amount of income a property could yield from rents, if all units were rented and all tenants paid their rent. This is typically not the case, so one must figure a vacancy as a collection loss. This is typically expressed as percentage of the potential gross income. The potential gross income less vacancy and collection loss is called the **effective gross income**. In determining the real rate of return on an income property, one must use the effective gross income as that amount represents the real dollars generated. After the effective gross income is determined, one subtracts the **annual operating expense**" to arrive at the **annual net operating income (NOI)**. The operating expenses include the fixed parts such as taxes, fire insurance, variable cost (i.e., utilities, maintenance, and replacement costs, appliances, carpet, etc.,) but do not include capital improvements, depreciation, or debt service. Once the annual NOI is determined, depreciation and debt service are deducted to arrive at the **internal rate of return (IRR)** before taxes or before cash flow. An investor would then consider their personal tax consequences to determine the internal rate of return after taxes. This is also referred to as the cash on cash return or after tax cash flow. The following is a basic cash flow summary: *(These are expenses in annual amounts.)*

		Potential Gross Income
(Less)	-	Vacancy and Collection Loss
		Effective Gross Income

		Effective Gross Income
(Less)	-	Operating Expenses
		Net Operating Income (NOI)

		Net Operating Income
(Less)	-	Depreciation and Debt Service
		Internal Rate of Return Before Taxes

		Internal Rate of Return Before Taxes
(Less)	-	Personal Tax Consequence
		Internal Rate of Return After Taxes
		(or Cash Flow After Taxes)

Now that we understand a basic cash flow for statements, let's look at capitalization problems. In our capitalization formula, we have annual net income; this is the same thing as net operating income.

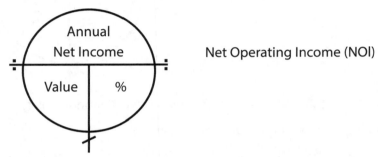

Net Operating Income (NOI)

1. The following information is available on a 10-unit apartment building with an annual gross potential rent of $57,500.

Vacancy rate 5%
Operating Expense $16,000
Depreciation $8,500
Debt Service $21,000

On the basis of the information above, what is the annual net operating income (NOI)?

a. $54,625
b. $38,625
c. $57,500
d. $16,000

Annual gross potential rent	$ 57,500	
Less vacancy rate	-$ 2,875	$57,500
		x 5%
Effective Gross Income	$54,625	$ 2,875
Effective Gross Income	$ 54,625	
Less Operating Expenses	-$ 16,000	
Annual Net Operating Income	$ 38,625	

Answer: B ($38,625)

2. An apartment building with 25 suites has a potential gross income of $97,500. The following information is available:

> Vacancy and collection loss 6%
>
> Operating Expenses $31,000
>
> Depreciation $9,150
>
> Debt Service $46,500

Based on the above information, what is the cash flow before taxes?

a. $60,650

b. $51,500

c. $5,850

d. $5,000

Answer: D ($5,000)

B. Conveyance Fee

The conveyance fee is also known as the transfer fee, auditor's fee. It is like a sales tax and paid by the seller at closing. For purposes of the exam, the conveyance fee is based on the sales price at the rate of 1 mill = 0.001 or 1/1000 of $1.00 or $1.00 per $1,000.

(a)   What is the county auditor's tax on a house that sold for $119,000?

Answer: $119

(b)   What is the transfer fee when a property sold for $75,900?

Answer: $75.90

(c)   What is the conveyance fee on a property that sold for $90,909?

Answer: $91.00 (goes to next highest dime)

C. % (Percent)of Profit

(a) A house that listed for $46,000 sold at 20% less than the list price. The buyer then turned around and sold for the list price. What was the % of profit?

1.   25%

2.   20%

3.   80%

4.   120%

The formula is: $$\frac{\text{WHAT YOU MADE}}{\text{WHAT YOU PAID}} = \text{\% OF PROFIT}$$

First: Let's figure out what he made.

The buyer bought the house for $46,000 less 20%:

$46,000 x 20% = $9,200

$46,000 - $9,200 = $36,800 (purchase price)

or, the buyer paid 80% of $46,000 = $36,800 (same answer)

The buyer then sold the house for $46,000:

$46,000   sales price
- $36.800   paid
$ 9,200   profit or what you made

$$\frac{\text{What Was Made}}{\text{What You Paid}} = \frac{\$ 9,200}{\$36,800} = 25\% \text{ profit}$$

Answer: #1 (25%)

(b)   Gallagher bought a parcel of land for $60,000. She subdivided the land into 8 lots of equal frontage and sold them for $30,000 each. What was the % of return on this original investment?

1.   3%
2.   300%
3.   30%
4.   3000%

First: Again, let's figure out what she made. She made 8 lots out of the parcel of land and sold them for $30,000 each.

8 lots x $30,000 = $240,000 gross revenue
She paid $60,000 for the parcel of land (her cost).

$240,000 gross revenue
-   $ 60,000 she paid
$180,000 profit or what was made

$$\frac{\text{What Was Made}}{\text{What Was Paid}} = \frac{\$180,000}{\$ 60,000} = 300\% \text{ Profit}$$

D. Points and Miscellaneous Financial Problems

1 Point = 1% of the loan amount, not the sales price! The seller must pay points on VA loans (on exam, real world all are negotiable), on other loans they (points) are negotiable.

1.   In making a loan of $50,000, how much would the lender charge the seller at closing if the interest rate was 11 1/4% and three points were charged?

    a. $1,500.00

    b. $7,125.00

    c. $ 150.00

    d. $ 712.50

> First: We only care about the points.
>
> Remember, we don't need the interest rate information.
>
> 1 point = 1% so, 3 points = 3%
>
> Answer: a (The loan amount $50,000 x 3% = $1,500)

2.   Your buyer contracts to build an $80,000 home and is taking out a loan for $64,000. How much will a 1 1/2% loan origination fee cost him?

    a. $1,200

    b. $ 960

    c. $9,600

    d. $2,160

> $64,000 x 1 1/2% = $960
>
> Answer: b ($960) Trick: We don't care how much the house cost to build.

E. Taxes

The formula for taxes is x ÷ x. Taxes are usually paid in arrears. Don't worry about real life. With exam tax problems, they'll tell you what isn't paid.

> Step 1: x, appraised value by assessed rate
>
> * Step 2: ÷ assessed rate by 1,000 or 100
>
> Step 3: x that # by tax rate

*Taxes will either be given in mills or so many dollars per 100. We'll start with a mill problem. If it's in mills, we divide 1,000, if in $100s by 100.

1.   A house in Summers Township is appraised for $68,000. The assessed rate is 35%. The tax levy in Summers Township is 5.2 mills. What is the yearly tax rate?

Step 1: Take the (appraised value) x (assessed rate) = (assessed value)

| $68,000 | x | 35% | = $23,800 |

Step 2: Since the problem is given in mills, we divide by 1,000:

| $23,800 | ÷ | 1,000 | = 23.8 |

| Step 3: | 23.8 | x | 5.2 mills | = $123.76 |

Let's try one using 100s:

2.   The tax rate in Revere County is $2.80 per $100 of assessed value. The assessed rate is 40%. What will the yearly tax be on a home valued at $98,000?

Step 1:	$98,000	x	40%	=	$39,200
Step 2:	$39,200	÷	100	=	392
Step 3:	392	x	$2.80	=	$1,097.60 yearly tax

Note: If a tax problem is given with various mills such as schools 20 mills, sewers 4.5 mills, streets 8.0 mills, then simply add all the mills together.

F. Insurance Problems

Insurance problems are figured almost the same as taxes.

1.   A home is insured for 85% of its value. The insurance rate for a one-year policy is $0.75 per $100 of insured value. What is the insurance rate for a two-year policy on a home valued at $105,000?

Step 1:	$105,000	x	85%	=	$89,250
Step 2:	$89,250	÷	100	=	$892.50
Step 3:	$892.50	x	$0.75	=	$669.375 per year

Don't forget, they asked for the cost of a two-year policy!

$669.375 x 2 years = $1,338.75

G. Proration Problems

To prorate a cost such as taxes or insurance is to split that cost appropriately between buyer and seller. To avoid mistakes, and for consistency, we always figure the seller's portion. Assume 30 days per month, 365 days per year. Most proration problems can be figured bi-monthly, 1/3 of a month, etc.

Step 1:   We make a timeline

Step 2:   Mark closing date

Step 3:   Count out time up to closing date

Step 4:   Prorate

Step 5:   Look at question and determine whose portion they are asking for

1. Taxes for 2014 were $570. If a house closes on August 15, 2014, how much would the seller owe?

    (a) First Make a timeline. The problem covers 2014 only and taxes are due from January through December so that's how our timeline is dated.

January 2014 |————————✗————————| December 2014

8-15-14

    Now, mark the closing date under your timeline.

Now, count out how much time has elapsed from January 1 to the closing date. Count it on your fingers. January, February, March, April, May, June, July "STOP!"—the month before it closes. You can't count all of August because it closes August 15th and that's only 1/2 of a month. So, it's 7 1/2 months.

    All we have to do now is find out how much 1 month of taxes are.

    One year taxes were $570 ÷ 12 months = $47.50 per month

    ($47.50 per month) x (7.5 months) = $356.25

Remember, we always prorate the seller's portion. Then, we look at the question and determine who they're asking us for. This question asked for the seller's portion, so we're okay.

    (b) Taxes on a property for 2013 and 2014 were $875 per year and have not been paid. The property transferred on 3-15-14. What was the buyer's share of taxes on closing?

    Step 1: Make a timeline. This problem covers 2 years, 2013 and 2014, so our timeline will be for 2 years.

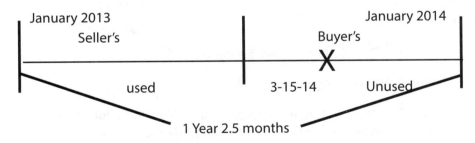

January 2013   January 2014

Seller's   Buyer's

✗

used   3-15-14   Unused

1 Year 2.5 months

    Step 2: Mark the closing date. (3-15-14)

    Step 3: Count out time from January 2013 through March 15, 2014. Hint: Figure all of 2013, so start counting from January of 2014. Jan., Feb., "STOP!" the month before it closes (only 1/2 of Feb.) 2.5 months. Don't forget the first year. Write 1 year 2.5 months under your timeline.

Step 4: If one year is $875,

$875 ÷ 12 = $72.92 per month x 2.5 months = 182.30

You're not done yet! Look under your timeline and add the one year

$875 + $189.29 = $1,057.30—Seller's portion

Step 5: Look at question—they want Buyer's share.

STOP! We don't have to re-prorate Buyer's portion, only subtract Seller's amount from the year; the difference is the Buyer's amount.

$875 x 2 years = $1,750 2/yrs. taxes $1,057.29 (seller's) = $692.70 (buyer's)

Answer: $692.70

(c) A seller prepaid a 3-year insurance policy on April 1, 2012. His insurance rate was based on 80% of his property value at $1.50 per $100 for 3 years. His property was appraised at $75,000. When he sold the house on September 1, 2014, the Buyer assumed the balance of the policy. What would the Seller's credit be?

First: Let's figure out how much the policy cost:

$75,000	x	80%	= $60,000
$60,000	÷	100	= $600
$ 600	x	$1.50	= $900 for 3 years

Step 1: Make a timeline (3-year timeline). Date each anniversary from when the policy started.

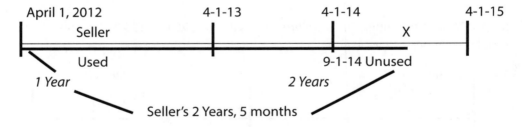

Step 2: Mark closing date (9-1-14)

Step 3: Start counting from here: All April, May, June, July, August... "STOP!" Nothing in September because the property closed 9-1-14 so it's 2 years, 5 months.

Step 4: $900 (for 3 years) ÷ 3 = $300 per year
                 $300 ÷ 12 months = $25/month x 5 months = $125
                 $300 per year x 2 years = $600
                 $600 + $125 = $725 Seller's portion

Step 5: The Seller's credit would be the Buyer's portion.

Total premium $900 - $725 (Seller's portion) = $175 Buyer's portion or Seller's Credit

H. Closing Statement

Currently the salesperson's exam **does not** include a closing statement problem, but we should have a basic understanding of how a closing statement is computed. When a property sells, both the buyer and the seller will have a closing or settlement statement prepared. This statement shows the accounting for the appropriate debits (expenses) and credits (income) for both parties.

The following is an example of a closing statement.

Closing Date:	August 20, 2014
Sale Price:	$65,000 buyer is putting 30% down and obtaining a second mortgage for $9,500
Commission:	7% of selling price (paid by seller)
Mortgage:	$36,000 principal balance with a 30-year note at 12% annual interest paid to June 1, 2014. The purchaser is assuming the unpaid balance of the seller's mortgage.
Insurance:	Prepaid 3-year premium was $370 commencing November 1, 2011
Taxes:	Land is valued at $12,000, improvements total $53,000. The real property is assessed at 35% of appraised value. The tax rate is $3.85 per $100. 2014 taxes have not been paid and will be due January 1, 2015.
Miscellaneous Costs:	$220 (Paid by seller from escrow. Conveyance fee included.)

1. What is the amount of credit due the buyer on tax proration?

Add land $12,000 + improvements $53,000 = $65,000

Now, it's just a regular tax problem.

$65,000	x	35%	= $22,750
$22,750	÷	100	= $ 227.50
$227.50	x	$3.85	= $ 875.88

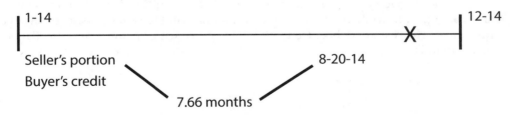

7 months + 20 days (20 days ÷ 30 days) = 7.66 months

$875.88 ÷ 12 mos. = $72.99 month x 7.66 months = $559.10

Who did they ask for? Buyer's credit which is the Seller's portion.

2. What is the amount of interest the seller will have to pay at closing?

> Figure 1-year interest first
>
> $36,000 x 12% = $4,320/annual interest
> $4,320 ÷ 12 = $360 interest per month
> $ 360 ÷ 30 = $12 per day
>
> The seller owes for June, July and 20 days in August
>
> $360 x 2.66 = $957.60   OR,
> $360 + $360 + $240 ($12 x 20 days) = $960

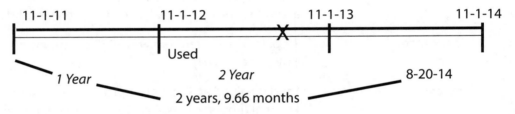

3. What will the seller's credit be for insurance proration?

> 3-year insurance policy was $370
> $370 ÷ 3 years =$123.33 per year
> $123.33 ÷ 12 = $10.28 per month

| 11-1-11 | 11-1-12 | 11-1-13 | 11-1-14 |

X

Used

1 Year   2 Year   8-20-14

2 years, 9.66 months

$123.33	x	2 years	=	$ 246.66
$ 10.28	x	9.66 months	=	$ 99.30
$246.66	+	$99.30	=	$ 345.96 seller used
$370	-	$345.96	=	$ 24.04 credit

4. What is the amount of the conveyance fee to be paid by the seller in this transaction?

$65,000 ÷ 1,000 = $65

5. What is the total commission?

$65,000 x 7% = $4,550

6. What is the net cash due the seller at closing?

The net cash due the seller is calculated by subtracting all of the debits or expenses from all of the credits or income. To figure this easily, one should draw a T-sheet. There are 7 items listed on a T-sheet for purposes of the state exam. To help you remember the items listed, read the notes given for the closing statement. If you're still an item short, read the question and you'll pick it up there. There are only 2 credits on the seller's T-sheet: Sales Price and Insurance. The rest are debits. Generally, conveyance fee is included in miscellaneous cost, read carefully.

	DEBITS (EXPENSES	CREDITS (INCOME)
Sales Price	—	$65,000.00
Commission	$4,550.00	—
Mortgage	$36,000.00	—
Interest	$ 960.00	—
Insurance	—	424.04
Taxes	$559.10	—
Misc. Costs	$ 220.00	—
TOTALS	$42,289.10	$65,024.04

Total Credits $65,024.04

Less Total Debits   <u>$42.289.10</u>

$22,734.94 Net cash due the seller on closing

I. Area Problems

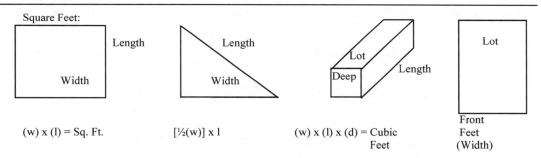

Square Feet:

Length

Width

(w) x (l) = Sq. Ft.

Length

Width

[½(w)] x l

Lot

Deep

Length

(w) x (l) x (d) = Cubic Feet

Lot

Front Feet (Width)

There are 43,560 sq. ft. in an acre, so...

Total Sq. Ft. ÷ 43,560 = # of Acres $\dfrac{\$}{\text{Land}}$ = Cost per sq. ft. (etc.)

# of Acres x 43,560 = sq. ft.

1. A lot that is 200 ft. wide x 580 ft. long is how many acres?

    First: Figure total sq. footage (area = width x length)

            200' x 580' = 116,000 sq. ft.

    Next: Total area in sq. ft. ÷ 43,560 = # of acres

            116,000 sq. ft. ÷ 43,560 = 2.66 acres

2. Simon bought 8.2 acres. How many sq. ft. did he buy?

    First: (# of acres) x (43,560) = sq. ft.

            8.2 acres x 43,560 = 357,192 sq. ft.

3. A lot that measures 85' wide by 100' deep is what fraction of an acre?

85' x 100' = 8,500 sq. ft.

8,500 sq. ft. ÷ 43,560 = 0.195

But all the answers are in fractions!

Remember: A fraction has a decimal equivalent

0.195 rounded up to 0.20 is 2/10 or 1/5.

Hint: Convert all answers into decimals

(a) 1/4 = 0.25 (b) 3/5 = 0.60
(c) 2/3 = 0.66 (d) 1/5 = 0.20

Now, which is the closest? That's right, "D"!

4. A buyer writes an offer to purchase some land 640' wide x 1,000' deep. His price is based on paying $1,500 per acre. How much is his offer for?

640' x 1,000' = 640,000 sq. ft.

640,000 ÷ 43,560 (sq. ft. in an acre) 14.69 acres

14.69 acres x $1,500 per acre = $22,035.00

5. A lot is 80' wide by 225' deep and sells for $4,500. How much is the sales price per sq. ft.?

Remember the formula: $$\frac{\$}{Land} = \text{Cost per sq. ft. (etc.)}$$

Figure the total sq. footage 80' x 225' = 18,000 sq. ft.

$$\frac{\$4,500}{18,000 \text{ sq. ft.}} = 0.25 \text{ or 25 cents per sq. ft.}$$

6. Rohl inherited the N 1/2 of the SW 1/4 of Section 23, Township 96, Range 52, of Turner County, South Dakota. How much more will he make if he divides the land into 50 lots and sells each for $2,500 than if he sells the land for $1,500 per acre?

First: We need to know how many acres he inherited. Remember, there are 640 acres in a section. Put 640 into your calculator and divide by the bottom #s, like this...

640 ÷ N1/2 ÷ SW1/4 = 80 Acres he inherited {640 ÷ 2 ÷ 4 = 80}

120,000
200,000

Now, by dividing the land into 50 lots, he will get:

50 lots x $2,500 = $125,000 gross revenue

By selling per acre, he will get:

80 acres x $1,500 = $120,000 gross revenue

$125,000 by lots $120,000 by acres = $5,000

He will make $5,000 more by selling the land as lots.

7. A developer owns 15 lots each 100' wide by 185' deep. He wants to make $112,500 from selling the lots. How much per front foot will the sale price be?

Remember: $$\frac{\$}{\text{Land}} = \text{cost per sq. ft. (etc.)}$$

First: Figure how many total front feet you have to work with.

Remember, front feet is the width of the lot (the first dimension given unless stated otherwise).

15 lots x 100 front feet = 1, 500 total front feet

$$\frac{\$112,500}{1,500 \text{ front feet}} = \$75 \text{ per front foot}$$

8. Your seller wants to list the above property for $1.95 per sq. ft. What will be the listing price?

First: Divide the parcel into rectangles and triangles like this: Then begin with each shape.

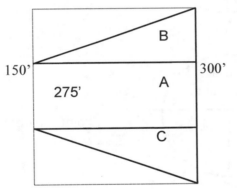

$$300'-150'=150' \div 2 = 75'$$

"A" RECTANGLE: 275' x 150' = 41,250 sq. ft.

"B" TRIANGLE: We need the dimension of the base. If we subtract 150' from the overall dimension of 300', what's left is divided between each triangle base.

The area of a right triangle is half the area of a rectangle.

75' x 275' = 20,625 sq. ft. ÷ 2 = 10,312.50 sq. ft.

"C" TRIANGLE: Same as "B"

Now add up all the sq. footages and multiply by $1.95

"A"	= 41,250	sq. ft +
"B"	= 10,312.50	sq. ft +
"C"	= 10,312.50	sq. ft.
	61,875	sq. ft.

61,875 sq. ft. x $1.95 per sq. ft. = $120,656.25 List Price

J. Panic Rules

Basic Pie

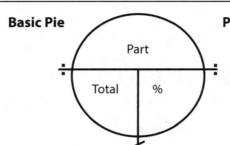

Panic Rule—"When in doubt, divide!"
* Divide little #s by big #s =%
* Divide little #s by % = big #s
* Big #s x % = little #s
"IS" means ÷ (divide)
"OF" means x (multiply)

Interest

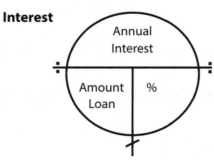

$\dfrac{\text{Made}}{\text{Paid}}$ = **% of Profit or Return**

$\dfrac{\text{Lost}}{\text{Cost}}$ = **% of Loss**

Capitalization

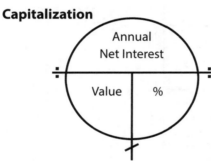

1 Point = 1% of Loan amount

1 Mill = 0.001 or $1/$1,000

Gross Rent Multiplier

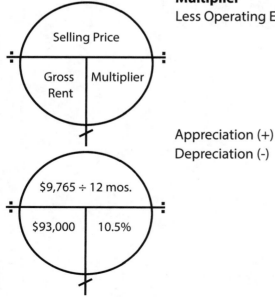

Potential Gross income
Less Vacancy and Collection Loss = Effective Gross Income
Less Operating Expenses = Net Operating Income

$\dfrac{\$}{\text{Land}}$ = **cost per Sq. Ft.; Acre; Cu. Foot**

43,560 sq. ft.	= **1 acre**
5,280'	= **1 mile**
36 sections	= **township**

Appreciation (+)
Depreciation (-)

640 acres = **1 section**
N1/4 SW1/2 = 640 ÷ 4 ÷ 2 = **# of acres**
9 sq. ft. = **1 sq. yd.**

Tax Formula x ÷ x
Appraised Value x Assessed Rate = Assessed Value
Assessed Value ÷ 100 or 1,000 = ?
? x Tax Rate = Yearly Tax

III. Math Formulas

1. Percentage Problems (Basic Pie)

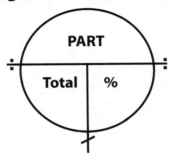

Part: Always a smaller number

Total: Always a larger number

Percent: Always a Percentage

Any two (2) known factors, you can arrive at third (3rd)

a.	Part	÷	Total	=	%	
b.	Part	÷	%	=	Total	
c.	Total	x	%	=	Part	

3 Golden Rules

2. Interest Problem

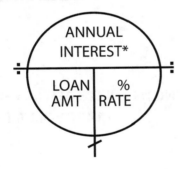

All factors must be expressed on an annual basis; if expressed monthly, the figure must be multiplied by 12.

If expressed quarterly, the figure must be multiplied by 4.

3. Capitalization Problems (Rate of Return)

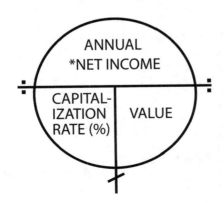

$$V \times R = I$$
$$I \div V = R$$
$$I \div R = V$$

Always Net Income (Rent)

4. Measurements

36 SECTIONS	=	1 TOWNSHIP	=	6 MILES x 6 MILES
640 ACRES	=	1 SECTION	=	1 MILE x 1 MILE
43,560 SQUARE FEET	=	1 ACRE		
5,280 FEET	=	1 MILE		

To locate a parcel of land, read legal description backwards.

To figure number (#) of acres, start with 640 and divide by bottom numbers.

Example: NW ¼ SW ¼ = 640 4 ÷ 4 = 40 Acres

5. Area Of Volume

a.   **FRONT** (A) x **DEPTH** (B) = **AREA OF A LOT** (Sq. Ft.)

Sq. Ft. : 43,560 = Number of Acres

Number of Acres x 43,560 = Sq. Ft.

If not otherwise specified, front footage is 1st dimension stated.

b.   **LENGTH** (A) x **WIDTH** (B) x **HEIGHT** (C) = **CUBIC VOLUME**

c.   **9** Square Feet = **1** Square Yard

d.   *Area is always expressed in square units. To compute triangular shaded area, Use*

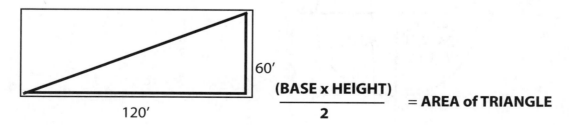

$$\frac{(\text{BASE} \times \text{HEIGHT})}{2} = \text{AREA of TRIANGLE}$$

Example: 60' x 120' = 7,200 sq. ft. ÷ 2 = 3,600 sq. ft.

6. Transfer Tax

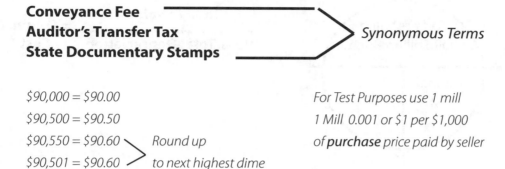

Conveyance Fee
Auditor's Transfer Tax
State Documentary Stamps

> *Synonymous Terms*

$90,000 = $90.00
$90,500 = $90.50
$90,550 = $90.60 ⟩ *Round up*
$90,501 = $90.60 ⟋ *to next highest dime*

For Test Purposes use 1 mill
1 Mill 0.001 or $1 per $1,000
*of **purchase** price paid by seller*

7. Tax Problems

(Appraised or Market Value) x (Assessed Rate) = **Assessed Value** (Assessed Value) ÷ (may be stated $$ per 100 or Mills = 1,000) = _____ x (Tax Rate) = **Yearly Taxes**

8. Insurance

(Appraised or Market Value) x (Insurance Rate) = **Insured Value** (Insured Value) ÷ (may be stated $$ per 100 or Mills = 1,000) = _____ x (Insurance Rate) = **Annual Premium**

9. Appreciation (+ "A" for Add)

$$\frac{\text{Today's Value}}{\text{Total Appreciation}} = \frac{\text{Original}}{\text{Cost}}$$

10. Depreciation ("D" for Deduct)

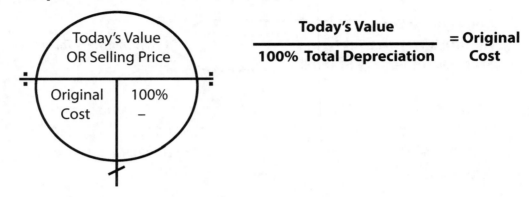

$$\frac{\text{Today's Value}}{100\% \ \text{Total Depreciation}} = \text{Original Cost}$$

11. Percentage of Profit/Loss

$$\frac{\text{What You Made}}{\textbf{What You Paid}} = \% \text{ of Profit}$$

$$\frac{\text{What You Lost}}{\textbf{What It Cost}} = \% \text{ of Loss}$$

12. Points

A **point** is defined as *1% of the loan/mortgage amount*.
Example: A $30,000 mortgage with **2** points charged is **$600**.

13. Potential Gross Income

Potential Gross Income **Less** Vacancy and Collection Loss **= Effective Gross Income**
Effective Gross Income **Less** Operating Expenses = **Net Operating Income**
Then use Capitalization Formula.

14. Net Problems

15. Gross Rent Multiplier

*Multiplier is a factor
Do not use % key

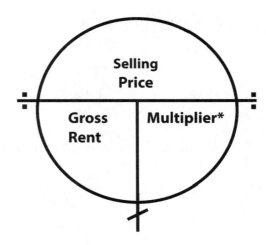

16. ProratIng

A.   Find closing date; if not date of close, use date of sale

B.   Decide *whether* an accrued (unpaid) or prepaid item

C.   Find cost per year, month, and day

D.   Find time in years, months, and/or days *

E.   Multiply "Time" by "Cost"

Calendar year method 365 Days Actual Days **or** Statutory method 360 Days 30 Day months (close counts on test)
Be sure to read problem; instructions should indicate which method.

17. Recapture Rate

Recapture rate is equal to the rate of depreciation that is allowed for 1 year. The rate is expressed as a % *not* in decimal form.

Example: 30 years = 1/30

1/30 = 0.0333 = 3.33%

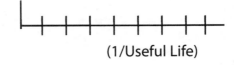

(1/Useful Life)

18. Ratios

Ratios are ways of comparing portions of a whole thing, and are simple fractions.

Example: **3** to **2** = 3/5 is (60%) of total and 2/5 is (40%) of total.

19. Miscellaneous

A.
$$\frac{\$\$}{\text{LAND}} = \begin{array}{l} \textbf{Cost per} \\ \textbf{Sq. Ft.} \\ \textbf{Acre} \\ \textbf{Cu. Ft.} \end{array}$$

B.   To convert fraction to decimal

Example: $2/3 = 2 \div 3 = $ **.6667**

C.   In simple problems, words translate into symbols:

   (1)   "of" means **x**

   (2)   "is" means ÷

D.   **When in doubt DIVIDE (÷)**

E.   Use the % key; will set decimal; Put **%** in calculator **last.**

F.   **Loan-to-value** ratio is the % of the property value that a lender will loan a borrower. Loan is based on the appraised or market value, whichever is *lower*.

G.   Gross and Net Profit

   (1)   Selling Price Cost = **Gross Profit**

   (2)   Gross Profit Expenses = **Net Profit**

H.   **Close counts on exam. Do NOT spend 20 minutes to find 5 cents.**

I.   **FINAL PANIC RULE**: Work problem *from right to left* by using given answers.

APPLICATION OF THE CIRCLE
TO THE SOLUTION OF MATH PROBLEMS

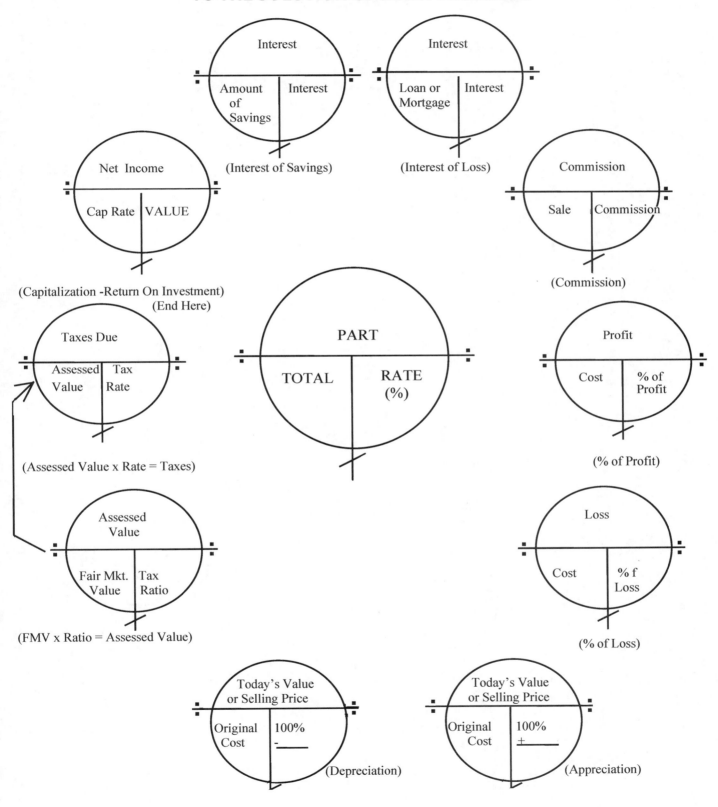

(Interest of Savings)

(Interest of Loss)

(Capitalization -Return On Investment)
(End Here)

(Assessed Value x Rate = Taxes)

(Commission)

(% of Profit)

(FMV x Ratio = Assessed Value)

(% of Loss)

(Depreciation)

(Appreciation)

Math Practice

Practice Test #1

1. **A sales associate has 1.65 acres of land listed at 20½ cents per square foot. What is the selling price?**
   a. $14,734.17
   b. $15,000.00
   c. $14,134.17
   d. $21,150.00

2. **The taxes for 2005 on a property were $345.00 and were paid by the owner. What refund would the owner get from a purchaser if the owner sold the house, and the taxes were prorated on October 15, 2005? (Use 30-day month.)**
   a. $77.28
   b. $71.88
   c. $70.15
   d. $273.12

3. **In making a loan of $25,000, how much would the lender charge the seller in discount points at closing if mortgages were being discounted 4½ points?**
   a. $ 375.65
   b. $1,125.00
   c. $ 725.60
   d. $ 900.00

4. **You have a listing on a house priced at $98,900. If the house sells for the listed price, the seller will make a gross profit of 15%. What did the house cost the seller?**
   a. $83,950.00
   b. $86,000.00
   c. $84,065.00
   d. $88,250.00

5. **A special tax levy is passed for 4.3 mills. Clark owns property with a market value of $72,000. Property is assessed for tax purposes at 40% of its appraised value. What will the 4.3 mill tax levy cost Clark yearly?**
   a. $134.40
   b. $123.84
   c. $309.60
   d. $ 56.60

6. **A real estate agency collected rents for one month, as follows: $160 each for 3 apartments; $175 each for 4 apartments; $185 each for 6 apartments. The month's expenses on this apartment building are: utilities $150 and repairs $75.80. If commission is five percent of the gross income, what is the agency's commission?**
   a. $ 95.80
   b. $125.60
   c. $114.50
   d. $103.21

7. **An investor purchased ten building lots for partial resale, each with a frontage of 75 feet, for $50,000. The investor wants to keep two lots for personal use and additionally make a profit of $25,000 on the resale. What must the sale price per front foot be on each lot sold?**
   a. $225
   b. $125
   c. $100
   d. $720

8. *A lender charged a 2% loan origination fee and three discount points to make a 95% conventional insured mortgage loan in the amount of $47,500. What was the cost of these charges to the borrower?*

a. $1,425

b. $1,118

c. $2,375

d. $ 922

9. *There is a balance of $24,350 due on a contract that requires monthly payments of $240, plus interest at a rate of 13.25% per annum. What is the amount of the next payment, including principal and interest?*

a. $ 654.25

b. $ 508.86

c. $3,226.38

d. $ 268.86

10. *In an apartment house with 12 apartments, rent is $100 per month, including utilities. If utilities cost an average of $1,994 per year for the apartment building, how much more is the owner netting than if the apartments rented for $82.50 per month without utilities?*

a. $1,245.60

b. $ 526.00

c. $ 756.00

d. $1,994.00

11. *Berger bought two adjacent lots, 50 feet W x 100 feet L and 100 feet W x 100 feet L, for a total of $9,000. They were later divided into three lots of equal frontage and sold for $4,000 each. What is the percent of return on the original investment?*

a. 25 percent

b. 50 percent

c. 33.33 percent

d. 75 percent

12. *Three-fifths (3/5) of the value of a property is $85,000. What is 75 percent of the value of the property (to the nearest dollar)?*

a. $ 51,000

b. $106,250

c. $141,667

d. $ 63,750

13. *Which of the following would yield a 10 percent capitalization rate?*

a. Net income of $8,000; sale price of $80,000

b. Gross income of $8,000; sale price of $80,000

c. Gross expense of $8,000; sale price of $80,000

d. Net expense of $8,000; sale price of $80,000

14. *You, a sales associate, are to receive 60% of the brokerage fee from the sale of a property. The property sold for $52,000. The fee is 7% on the first $30,000 and 3½% on the remaining amount. What commission will you receive?*

a. $1,925

b. $1,148

c. $2,870

d. $1,722

15. *A property has a gross annual income of $14,250 and monthly expenses of $300. It has been valued at $147,000. What is the capitalization rate?*

a. 7.2 percent

b. 9.6 percent

c. 6.1 percent

d. 5.4 percent

16. *Compute the total cost of the following property: Land 125 feet x 100 feet @ $1.00 per square foot; two-story building 40 feet x 60 feet @ $25.00 per square foot; full basement 40 feet x 60 feet @ $5.00 per square foot; driveway 10 feet x 80 feet @ $4.00 per square foot; sidewalk 3 feet x 70 feet @ $3.00 per square foot.*

a. $148,330

b. $ 93,336

c. $153,330

d. $140,830

17. **A home is covered by a three-year fire insurance policy that expires July 11, 2004. The premium paid was $489. The home was sold and the closing was on September 23, 2003. How much money is credited to the seller at closing if the policy is assumed by the purchaser (based on 30-day month)?**

a. $124.65

b. $130.40

c. $138.10

d. $118.18

18. **The listing price of a house is $46,000. You bought it for the listing price less 20% and sold it for the listing price. What percent of profit did you make?**

a. 80%

b. 6%

c. 25%

d. 20%

19. **Your client leases a storeroom on a percentage basis. The lease calls for a minimum rental of $300 per month and 5% of the gross annual sales over $80,000. How much is the annual rent with a gross annual business of $150,000?**

a. $7,500

b. $3,500

c. $3,600

d. $7,100

20. **A home has a present depreciated value of $36,900. What was its original cost if it has depreciated at a rate of 2¼% for the past 8 years? (Straight-line basis depreciation.)**

a. $36,900

b. $49,600

c. $43,875

d. $45,000

21. **If a house sold for $69,120 at a loss of 4%, what was the original cost of the house?**

a. $72,000.00

b. $49,600.00

c. $66,355.20

d. $71,500.00

22. **A seller advises a broker that the seller must net $24,000 from the sale of a property. There is an existing mortgage of $94,500, the agreed commission is 4½%, and miscellaneous closing costs will be $4,350. What is the least amount that the property can sell for and return the seller's desired amount?**

a. $127,508

b. $124,083

c. $128,639

d. $128,378

23. **The mortgage loan on a house is $9,500. Monthly interest and amortization of principal required at $9.50 per $1,000 loan. Annual taxes are $291. Fire and extended coverage insurance rate is $0.98 per $100 on a three year policy in the amount of the original loan. What is the total monthly payment to be made on interest, principal, taxes, and insurance?**

a. $ 98.00

b. $117.09

c. $111.09

d. $131.17

24. **Chris wants to build a patio 60 feet x 20 feet and 4 inches thick. How many cubic yards of concrete will be needed?**

a. 14.8

b. 12.4

c. 120

d. 400

25. **If a building has an estimated remaining economic life of 35 years, the appropriate recapture rate will be:**

a. 2.75%

b. 2.5%

c. 2.86%

d. 3.33%

26. **A home is appraised at $125,000. The assessment level is 35%. There is a total of 40 mills in the taxing area. What are the monthly taxes on the home?**

a. $1,750.00

b. $ 466.66

c. $ 145.83

d. $2,360.64

27. **A building was sold for $20,000. Earnest money of $2,000 was deposited and the buyer obtained a loan for the remainder. The mortgage broker charged a fee of one "point." What was the total cash used by the buyer for the purchase?**

a. $2,760
b. $2,180
c. $ 180
d. $18,180

28. **A house sold for $35,550, which was 11% more than the original cost of the house. The original cost of the house was:**

a. $33,000
b. $32,000
c. $32,027
d. $33,037

29. **A transaction closed July 1, 2004. Insurance for three years was taken out April 1, 2004. The prepaid three-year premium was $375. What credit should the seller receive on the proration of the insurance?**

a. $ 31.36
b. $293.75
c. $343.76
d. $375.00

30. **A rectangular lot 330 feet long and 210 feet wide was subdivided into 6 lots of 110' x 90' with a road running lengthwise through the middle of the lot. How many square feet are required for the road?**

a. 8,100 sq. ft.
b. 9,000 sq. ft.
c. 9,900 sq. ft.
d. 10,000 sq. ft.

Practice Test #2

1. **Judi Pea, a broker, sold a home. The commission rate was 7%. Judi gave Freddie Bahr, a salesperson, half of the $2,380 gross commission. What was the selling price of the home?**

a. $43,000
b. $25,466
c. $34,000
d. $68,000

2. **If a mortgage on a house is 80% of the appraised value and the mortgage interest of 8% amounts to $460 per month, what is the appraised value of the house?**

a. $86,250
b. $71,875
c. $69,000
d. $92,875

3. **If the quarterly interest at 7.5% is $562.50, what is the principal amount of the loan?**

a. $ 7,500
b. $75,000
c. $30,000
d. $90,000

4. **The mortgagor computed the interest that was charged for the previous month on a $60,000 mortgage loan balance as $412.50. What is the rate of interest?**

a. 7½%
b. 7¾%
c. 8¼%
d. 8½%

5. **A broker holds a listing on a vacant lot, measuring 100 feet wide and 125 feet deep, at a listing price of $250 per front foot. The commission that the broker will collect on the transaction is set in the listing agreement at 8%. If the property sells for its full asking price, what will the broker's fee be?**

a. $2,500
b. $2,000
c. $1,500
d. $1,250

6. **Jones wishes to net $96,000 after deducting an 8% commission from the selling price of a home. What must the selling price be to accommodate Jones?**
   a. $112,800
   b. $134,680
   c. $104,348
   d. $103,680

7. **If the annual rate of interest on a mortgage loan is 8½%, and the monthly interest payment is $201.46, what is the principal amount of the loan?**
   a. $2,417.52
   b. $28,441.41
   c. $2,844.14
   d. $14,270.00

8. **One of broker Millie's salespeople sold a house for $82,000. Millie received 48% of the commission and paid the salesperson 55% of that amount. How much did Millie keep, if the commission rate is 7%?**
   a. $2,755.20
   b. $1,515.36
   c. $1,239.84
   d. $3,157.00

9. **A building was sold for $60,000. The buyer put up 10% in cash and obtained a loan for the balance. The lending institution charged a 1% loan origination fee. What was the total cash used by the buyer for this purchase?**
   a. $6,540
   b. $6,600
   c. $540
   d. $6,000

10. **A home has a present depreciated value of $36,900. What was its original cost if it has depreciated at a rate of 2¼% a year for the past 8 years?**
    a. $36,900
    b. $49,600
    c. $43,875
    d. $45,000

11. **An investor bought a parcel of unimproved land that appreciated in value 12% a year for three years. At the end of that time, the land was sold for $21,760. What was the original purchase price?**
    a. $16,000
    b. $18,500
    c. $20,500
    d. $14,700

12. **A property has a gross annual income of $14,250 and monthly expense of $300. It has been valued at $147,000. What is the capitalization rate?**
    a. 7.2%
    b. 9.6%
    c. 2.42%
    d. 5.4%

13. **The Monroe's home is valued at $65,000. Property in their area is assessed at 60% of its value, and the local tax rate is $2.85 per hundred. What are the Monroe's monthly taxes?**
    a. $1,111.50
    b. $ 926.30
    c. $ 111.15
    d. $ 92.63

14. **If the market value of a house is $84,500, the assessment ratio is 35%, and the tax rate is 30 mills, what are the monthly taxes?**
    a. $887.25
    b. $942.50
    c. $ 73.94
    d. $ 87.72

15. **An insurance premium has been paid in advance by the seller on a house. The policy, worth $50,000, has a premium of $400 for a three-year period, beginning January 1, 2002. The closing date for the sale of the home is July 15, 2003. The amount to be reimbursed is:**
    a. $194.46
    b. $205.46
    c. $201.58
    d. $ 95.89

16. **A building is sold for $90,000. At the time of closing, credit is given to the purchaser for a $15,000 first mortgage and $10,000 second mortgage existing on the property. What amount of a 1-mill transfer fee must be paid?**

    a. $ 45.00
    b. $900.00
    c. $ 90.00
    d. $ 65.00

17. **A 2.6-acre lot sold for $188,000. What was the price per square foot?**

    a. $1.19
    b. $1.55
    c. $1.66
    d. $1.82

18. **Find the area of the lot illustrated below. (Not to scale.)**

    a. 3,800 sq. ft.
    b. 4,000 sq. ft.
    c. 4,200 sq. ft.
    d. 3,600 sq. ft.

19. **What would it cost to lay a new floor in a den measuring 15 feet by 20 feet if the cost of materials is $6.95 per square yard and the cost of labor is an additional $250?**

    a. $ 231.67
    b. $ 481.67
    c. $ 610.33
    d. $2,335.00

20. **How many acres are in the NE 1/4 of the SE 1/4 plus the N 1/2 of the SW 1/4?**

    a. 120 acres
    b. 5 acres
    c. 10 acres
    d. 20 acres

21. **Which of the following descriptions is the proper one for the shaded area?**

    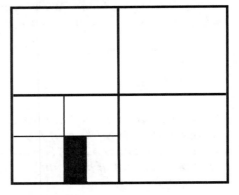

    a. W 1/2 of the SE 1/4 of the SW 1/4
    b. S 1/2 of the SW 1/4 of the SE 1/4
    c. E 1/2 of the SW 1/4 of the SW 1/4
    d. W 1/2 of the SE 1/4 of the SE 1/4

22. **Betsy's Spa lease requires $300 per month rent plus 6% of the gross receipts. Last month, gross receipts totaled $2,450. How much rent did Betsy pay last month?**

    a. $147
    b. $300
    c. $447
    d. $347

23. **A property sold for $40,625 with an 80% loan at 9% interest. If the monthly payment is $325, what is the remaining balance on the loan at the end of 2 months?**

    a. $32,337
    b. $40,584
    c. $40,605
    d. $32,419

24. **A commercial property producing an annual gross income of $39,000 was sold two months ago for $341,250. The property's gross rent multiplier is:**

    a. 7.0
    b. 7.75
    c. 8.5
    d. 8.75

25. **How many cubic feet are in a storage area 15 yards wide, 15 feet deep, and 12 feet high?**

    a. 2,700 cubic feet
    b. 225 cubic feet
    c. 8,100 cubic feet
    d. 675 cubic feet

26. **A buyer's closing statement shows different items including a purchase price of $37,000, first mortgage $24,000, second mortgage $4,000, total debits $38,608.06, taxes $458, title insurance $350, total credits $34,370, proration of rents $250, and earnest deposit of $1,000. Based on this information, determine the balance due the seller from the buyer.**

    a. $5,550.42
    b. $6,385.25
    c. $4,238.06
    d. $7,850.00

27. **A purchaser agrees to buy a house for $47,000, obtaining a 90% loan and making a deposit of $2,500. If attorney fees are $225, how much will the buyer need to bring to closing?**

    a. $4,700
    b. $44,725
    c. $42,525
    d. $2,425

28. **A land developer wants to divide a 15-acre tract of land into lots that are 50 feet x 120 feet each. If the developer allowed 50,000 square feet for streets, how many lots can be developed in the subdivision?**

    a. 104
    b. 102
    c. 100
    d. 101

29. **Perry White got a second mortgage for $1,500 at 9% interest only for two years. What was the amount of principal due?**

    a. $1,230
    b. $1,365
    c. $1,500
    d. $1,770

30. **The Sheets, who own their house free of any encumbrance, are selling it to the Irwins for $145,000. The purchase price is to be paid by the Irwins, earnest money deposit of $3,000, and their cash payment of $42,000, with the Sheets taking back an amortized loan on the house for $100,000 at 12% interest for 15 years. This mortgage arrangement is best described as:**

    a. Junior mortgage
    b. Partially amortized mortgage
    c. Wraparound mortgage
    d. Purchase money mortgage

Answer Key: Math Practice

Practice Test #1 Answers

1........a	13.......a	25.......c
2.......b	14.......d	26.......c
3.......b	15.......a	27.......b
4.......b	16.......a	28.......c
5.......b	17.......b	29.......c
6.......c	18.......c	30.......c
7.......b	19.......d	
8.......c	20.......d	
9.......b	21.......a	
10.......b	22.......c	
11.......c	23.......b	
12.......b	24.......a	

Practice Test #2 Answers

1.......c	13.......d	25.......c
2.......a	14.......c	26.......c
3.......c	15.......a	27.......d
4.......c	16.......c	28.......c
5.......b	17.......c	29.......c
6.......c	18.......c	30.......d
7.......b	19.......b	
8.......c	20.......a	
9.......a	21.......a	
10.......d	22.......c	
11.......a	23.......a	
12.......a	24.......d	

Sample Real Estate Exams

Real Estate Exam #1

1. **After a purchaser signs a sales contract, the salesperson must do which of the following?**
   a. Keep the original contract and give the purchaser a copy the next day
   b. Give the purchaser a copy immediately
   c. Mail the purchaser a copy after the statutory 3-day cooling off period
   d. None of the above

2. **Describing property by degrees, feet, and monuments is called:**
   a. Maps and plats system
   b. Rectangular survey system
   c. Metes and bounds system
   d. Lot and block system

3. **Which numbered area illustrates the location of the NE 1/4 of the SE 1/4 of the NW 1/4 of the section?**
   a. Area 2
   b. Area 1
   c. Area 4
   d. Area 3

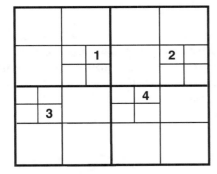

4. **How many acres are found in a description that reads: "the S 1/2 of the SW 1/4 of NE 1/4 and the N 1/2 of the NW 1/4 of the SE 1/4 of section 13?"**
   a. 20 acres
   b. 40 acres
   c. 80 acres
   d. 160 acres

5. **When land is taken under the right of eminent domain, which of the following must apply?**
   a. The statute of limitations must pass
   b. The taking must be for a public purpose
   c. The element of adverse possession must exist
   d. The government must give constructive notice

6. **Brown owns a large parcel of undeveloped land, in severalty. Fuller, a developer, enters an agreement with Brown to purchase the property. Fuller insists that Brown's wife also sign the deed along with her husband. Fuller is trying to:**
   a. Arrange a sale-leaseback agreement
   b. Comply with the law of courtesy
   c. Terminate any rights Mrs. Brown may have in the property
   d. Subordinate Mrs. Brown's interest in the property to his own

7. **A defect or a cloud on the title to property is best cured by:**
   a. Quitclaim deed from all parties who may have an interest in the property
   b. A partition action
   c. Obtaining title insurance
   d. Repudiating adverse claims

8. **Which one of the following is not real property?**
   a. Wall-to-wall carpeting installed over plywood subfloor
   b. Built-in dishwasher
   c. Drapes
   d. Sump pump

9. **An unlicensed secretary for a property manager can only do which of the following tasks?**
   a. Collect rents
   b. Publish a listing
   c. Take a listing
   d. Negotiate a lease contract

10. **Adams possesses Wilson's property for 15 years with Wilson's permission. Adams then claims title under the law of adverse possession. Which of the following statements is true?**
    a. Adams will succeed because he possessed the property continuously for more than the required period
    b. Adams will succeed because he paid the taxes during the required period
    c. Adams will not succeed because 15 years is not long enough to satisfy the statute of limitations.
    d. Adams will not succeed because not all of the requirements for title by adverse possession have been satisfied

11. **All of the following are examples of a specific lien, except:**
    a. Property taxes
    b. Judgment
    c. Mechanic's lien
    d. Mortgage

12. **The primary difference between a general and a specific lien is:**
    a. A general lien affects all of a debtor's property; a specific lien does not
    b. A specific lien affects all of a debtor's property; a general lien does not
    c. Specific and general liens are the same as a judgment lien
    d. A general lien is less binding than a specific lien

13. **A home is appraised at $125,000. The assessment level is 35%. There are a total of 40 mills in the taxing area. What are the monthly taxes on the home?**
    a. $1,750.00
    b. $ 466.66
    c. $2,360.64
    d. $ 145.83

14. **Which of the following describes an ordinary life estate?**
    a. A homestead
    b. An estate granted for the grantee's lifetime
    c. An estate granted for the grantor's lifetime
    d. A remainder interest

15. **Baker conveys a life estate to her grandson and stipulates that upon her grandson's death the title will pass to her nephew. What is the nephew's interest called?**
    a. Estate in reversion
    b. Estate for years
    c. Estate in remainder
    d. Periodic estate

16. **A contract agreed to under duress is:**
    a. Voidable
    b. Breached
    c. Discharged
    d. Void

17. **An investor borrowed $28,000 at 10% interest and repaid the loan in 15 months. How much money was repaid to the nearest $100?**
    a. $30,800
    b. $38,800
    c. $31,500
    d. $42,000

18. **After the snowstorm of the century, Frank Simpson offers to pay $60.00 to whoever will shovel his driveway. This is an example of which of the following?**

    a. An implied contract
    b. A bilateral contract
    c. A license
    d. A unilateral contract

19. **All of the following will terminate an offer, except:**

    a. Revocation of the offer before acceptance
    b. Death of the offeror before acceptance
    c. A counter offer by the offeree
    d. An offer from a third party

20. **X listed a property. X finds a buyer. Can X write an offer as a buyer's representative?**

    a. Yes, if explicitly stated in the contract and agreed to by both buyer and seller
    b. Yes, you only need to have a buyer broker agreement in place
    c. No, you cannot collect both commissions
    d. No, it is against the Federal Antitrust Laws

21. **What is steering?**

    a. Leading prospective homeowners to or away from certain areas
    b. Refusing to make loans in certain areas because of their ethnic makeup
    c. Suggesting an owner should sell now because property values are expected to decline as more and more minorities infiltrate the area
    d. Refusing to help prospective buyers locate housing because of their race, color, creed, national origin, handicap, or familial status

22. **Which of the following is an example of blockbusting?**

    a. Despite the all-white character of a neighborhood and the implication the seller would like to see it remain that way, the broker insists on showing the property to several non-white buyers who've expressed an interest in the area
    b. A broker moves a minority person into a neighborhood with the intent of buying other houses in the neighborhood at greatly reduced prices
    c. A salesperson shows a minority client only properties in areas mostly populated by the same minority
    d. A bank refuses to lend to residents of certain neighborhoods because of their racial makeup

23. **If a salesperson is taking a listing and the seller states that he wishes to sell only to members of a particular race, the salesperson should:**

    a. Comply with the seller's wishes
    b. Refuse to take the listing
    c. Take the listing but ignore the seller's request
    d. Say he must consult with his broker before making a decision

24. **If a spouse owns a parcel of land separately, the spouse is said to own it:**

    a. As a joint tenant
    b. As a tenant in common
    c. As a tenant by the entireties
    d. In severalty

25. **All of the following are true statements about a joint tenancy, except:**

    a. It is created only when four unities are present
    b. It cannot be created by operation of law
    c. A joint tenant's interest can be willed to heirs
    d. There exists a right of survivorship

26. **A joint tenancy is created:**

    a. Automatically, if the property is distributed by the court to surviving heirs
    b. By presumption, if the method of ownership is not stipulated
    c. By deed or by will
    d. By deed only

27. **Turner and Myers are joint tenants. Turner sells her interest to Smith. What is the relationship between Myers and Smith?**
    a. They are joint tenants
    b. They are tenants in common
    c. They each own an interest in severalty
    d. Their relationship must be described in the deed

28. **Which of the following is *not* an example of a common area of a condominium?**
    a. Laundromat
    b. Designated parking space
    c. Swimming pool
    d. The land

29. **Simon buys into a cooperative apartment building. Under this form of ownership:**
    a. Simon will become a stockholder in a corporation or a shareholder in an association
    b. Simon will receive a deed for his interest in the cooperative
    c. The value of Simon's interest in the cooperative will be assessed separately and a tax bill will be sent directly to Simon
    d. Simon will receive a 25-year lease for the unit

30. **Bart Buyer purchases a house for $77,500. The loan requires a 15% down payment, an origination fee of 0.75%, 2.25 discount points, and a 0.5% PMI fee. How much money does Bart need to close this transaction?**
    a. $ 7,750.00
    b. $13,930.63
    c. $ 9,665.25
    d. $14,337.50

31. **Gray bought a house from Green. Green agreed to take $605/month for the next 7 years. The total balance will be due, and legal title will change hands at that time. This is a:**
    a. Blanket mortgage
    b. Purchase-money mortgage
    c. Wraparound mortgage
    d. Land contract

32. **A lease is affected in which of the following ways when the lessor dies?**
    a. It is void
    b. It is terminated
    c. It can be terminated by the lessee
    d. It is not affected in any way

33. **A lease under which the tenant pays taxes, maintenance, and insurance costs, as well as a fixed monthly rental, is known as:**
    a. A gross lease
    b. A net lease
    c. A percentage lease
    d. A graduated lease

34. **In a sale-and-leaseback arrangement:**
    a. The seller retains title to the real estate
    b. The buyer gets possession of the property
    c. The seller retains possession of the property
    d. The buyer receives equitable title only

35. **Taxes levied on a property owner to pay for improvements that benefit only that property are called:**
    a. Fees
    b. General property taxes
    c. Special excise taxes
    d. Special assessments

36. **Tax assessment based on the value of a property is known as which of the following?**
    a. Appraisal
    b. Ad valorem
    c. Replacement cost
    d. Accretion

37. **If a mortgage on a property is 80% of the appraised value and the mortgage interest of 8% amounts to $460 per month, what is the appraised value of the house?**
    a. $86,250
    b. $71,875
    c. $69,000
    d. $92,875

38. *The market price of real estate is generally the same as:*

  a. Sales price

  b. Appraised value

  c. Highest and best use

  d. Mortgage loan value

39. *The market value of a piece of land is the:*

  a. Present value future benefits

  b. Actual cost to build

  c. Price paid by a buyer

  d. Market price

40. *A house with outmoded plumbing is suffering from:*

  a. Functional obsolescence

  b. Deferred maintenance

  c. Economic obsolescence

  d. Incurable physical deterioration

41. *In estimating the value of commercial property, what is the appraiser's most important consideration?*

  a. Its reproduction cost

  b. Its net income

  c. Its gross rent multiplier

  d. Its gross income

42. *Which of the following processes is used in the income approach to value?*

  a. Equalization

  b. Capitalization

  c. Amortization

  d. Depreciation

43. *Capitalization rates are:*

  a. Determined by the gross rent multiplier

  b. Determined by the amount of depreciation on the property

  c. A mathematical value of a property determined by the sale price

  d. The rates of return a property will produce on the owner's investment

44. *The gross monthly rent multiplier falls under which of the following appraisal methods:*

  a. Income approach

  b. Cost approach

  c. Sales comparison approach

  d. Competitive market analysis

45. *Reconciliation is an appraisal term used to describe:*

  a. Appraiser's determination of a property's highest value

  b. An average of real estate values for properties similar to the subject

  c. Appraiser's analysis and comparison of results of each appraisal approach

  d. Method used to determine a property's most appropriate capitalization rate

46. *Police powers include all of the following, except:*

  a. Zoning

  b. Liens

  c. Building codes

  d. Subdivision regulations

47. *A mortgage note must be:*

  a. A negotiable instrument

  b. Signed by the mortgagor

  c. Signed by the mortgagee

  d. Recorded to be valid

48. *A deed of trust gives title to the secured property to the:*

  a. Lender

  b. Trustor

  c. Trustee

  d. Seller

49. *A deed of trust creates a trust for which the:*

  a. Public records do not indicate the beneficial owner's identity

  b. Time limit is usually 25 years

  c. Time limit is l0 years

  d. None of the above

50. *Ling defaulted on the mortgage payments and the lender began a foreclosure action. At the foreclosure sale, Ling's house sold for only $75,000 while the unpaid balance on the loan was $86,000. What can the lender do about the $11,000 difference?*

  a. Sue for monetary damages

  b. Sue for injunctive relief

  c. Sue for specific performance

  d. Sue for a deficiency judgment

51. **White defaulted and the property was sold under foreclosure proceedings at a sheriff's sale. The period of time after the sale when White has the right to regain an interest in the property is known as the:**
   a. Equitable redemption period
   b. Statutory redemption period
   c. Information redemption period
   d. Formal redemption period

52. **The person who gets a real estate loan by signing a note and mortgage is the:**
   a. Mortgagor
   b. Mortgagee
   c. Optionor
   d. Optionee

53. **Discount points are:**
   a. Limited by government regulations
   b. Determined by the FHA
   c. Only charged on conventional loans
   d. Determined by the market

54. **Which of the following is true about an interest-only term mortgage?**
   a. All interest is paid at the end of the term
   b. The entire principal is due at the end of the term
   c. The entire debt is partially amortized over the term
   d. The term is limited by state regulation.

55. **The Boyd's bought their home three years ago. They made a $20,000 down payment and have paid $14,400 in mortgage payments over the last three years, $10,000 of which went to interest. The $24,400 invested in the home is referred to as their:**
   a. Homestead
   b. Profit
   c. Redemption
   d. Equity

56. **A government-sponsored loan that insures lenders against loss is a/an:**
   a. FHA mortgage
   b. VA mortgage
   c. Adjustable-rate mortgage
   d. Conventional mortgage

57. **All of the following agencies operate in the secondary market, except:**
   a. The Federal National Mortgage Association
   b. The Federal Savings Mortgage Association
   c. The Government National Mortgage Association
   d. The Federal Home Loan Mortgage Corporation

58. **All of the following are required by the Real Estate Settlement Procedures Act, except:**
   a. Lender must provide borrowers with a good faith estimate of closing costs
   b. A uniform settlement statement must be used in loan closings
   c. The borrower must be given five days to back out of the loan transaction after receiving the settlement statement
   d. No kickbacks may be given to any party in connection with the loan

59. **The Federal Truth in Lending Law:**
   a. Requires a lender to estimate a borrower's approximate loan closing costs before accepting a loan application
   b. Regulates advertising that contains information regarding mortgage terms
   c. Prevents broker from using phrase like "FHA financing available" in any ads
   d. Dictates that mortgage applications be made on specific government forms

60. **What type of mortgage allows a buyer to get financing from a seller without assuming the seller's first mortgage?**
   a. A wraparound mortgage
   b. An open end mortgage
   c. A balloon payment mortgage
   d. An accelerated mortgage

61. **When a mortgage loan requires periodic payments that will not fully amortize the amount of the loan by the final payment date, the final payment is called a/an:**
   a. Release payment
   b. Balloon payment
   c. Level payment
   d. Accelerated payment

62. **A mortgage instrument may include a clause that would prevent the assumption of the mortgage by a new purchaser. This is called a/an:**
    a. Alienation clause
    b. Power of sale clause
    c. Defeasance clause
    d. Acceleration clause

63. **In a lien theory state the:**
    a. Mortgagee takes title to mortgaged property during the term of a mortgage
    b. Mortgagor has a lien against a property for the full amount of the mortgage
    c. Mortgagor may foreclose only by court action
    d. Mortgagor holds title to the property during the term of the mortgage

64. **A lender who refuses to make loans in a specific area due to its racial makeup is guilty of:**
    a. Panic selling
    b. Blockbusting
    c. Steering
    d. Redlining

65. **When a sales contract form has only been signed by a purchaser and given to the seller's broker with an earnest money check:**
    a. This constitutes a valid contract
    b. The purchaser can sue the seller for specific performance
    c. This is considered on offer
    d. The earnest money belongs to the seller

66. **An offer may be terminated by:**
    a. Withdrawal by the purchaser
    b. A counteroffer by the seller
    c. The death of the offeror
    d. All of the above

67. **If the seller in a real estate contract breaches the contract, the buyer may:**
    a. Sue for damages
    b. Sue for specific performance
    c. Do nothing
    d. Do any of the above

68. **An option is a contract that:**
    a. Specifies a time limit within which to buy or lease a piece of property
    b. Is a bilateral, executory agreement
    c. Does not set the sale price
    d. Transfers title when signed

69. **Someone who engages another to act for him or her is called a/an:**
    a. Principal
    b. Grantor
    c. Testator
    d. Agent

70. **What is the relationship of brokers to their sellers?**
    a. Subagents
    b. Trustees
    c. Fiduciaries
    d. Attorneys-in-fact

71. **The rights of the owner with property abutting the bank of a stream are called:**
    a. Littoral rights
    b. Riparian rights
    c. Avulsion
    d. Dominant tenements

72. **Calvin purchased a waterfront property and shortly thereafter noticed that several people jogged along his beach every day. He inquired and learned that this had been a local practice for decades. Calvin took the matter to court to obtain an injunction preventing the joggers from crossing his property in the future. Calvin will probably:**
    a. Succeed, because the joggers are trespassing
    b. Succeed, because the joggers only have a license, which can be revoked
    c. Fail, because public riparian rights allow access to all beach front property
    d. Fail, because an easement by implication right has likely been acquired

73. *A building was sold for $20,000. Earnest money of $2,000 was deposited and the buyer obtained a loan for the remainder. The mortgage broker charged a fee of one point. What was the total cash used by the buyer for purchase?*

   a. $ 2,760
   b. $ 2,180
   c. $ 180
   d. $18,180

74. *A house sold for $35,550, which was 11% more than the original cost of the house. The original cost of the house was?*

   a. $33,000
   b. $32,000
   c. $32,027
   d. $33,037

75. *When real estate agents receive an earnest money deposit, the money must be:*

   a. Deposited into the agent's own trust account until the agent has time to deposit the money into the broker's trust account
   b. Deposited into the broker's trust account
   c. Held in the broker's safe until transaction is consummated
   d. None of the above

76. *During periods of rising interest rates, which clause in a mortgage is most beneficial to the mortgagor if the loan is one with an adjustable rate?*

   a. Alliteration
   b. Acceleration
   c. Prepayment
   d. Escalator

77. *The real estate broker or salesperson needs to have:*

   a. Little understanding of law because competent attorneys are available
   b. A broad understanding of law and how it affects real estate
   c. Legal experience as a practicing attorney
   d. An in-depth understanding of constitutional law

78. *A transaction was closed July 1, 2003. Insurance for three years was taken out April 1, 2003 and the prepaid three-year premium was $375. What credit should the seller receive on the proration of the insurance?*

   a. $ 31.36
   b. $293.75
   c. $343.76
   d. $375.00

79. *A rectangular lot 330 feet long and 210 feet wide was subdivided into 6 lots of 110' x 90' with a road running lengthwise through the middle of the lot. How many square feet are required for the road?*

   a. 8,100 sq. ft
   b. 9,000 sq. ft
   c. 9,900 sq. ft
   d. 10,000 sq. ft

80. *Which of the following can a real estate licensee prepare for another broker for a fee?*

   a. The contract for sale
   b. A deed
   c. A land contract
   d. None of the above because that would be unauthorized practice of law

81. *Real estate license laws were established:*

   a. For political reasons only
   b. To protect the public
   c. To protect new salespersons
   d. To raise revenues for the state

82. *A buyer's closing statement shows different items, including a purchase price of $37,000, first mortgage $24,000, second mortgage $4,000, total debits $38,608.06, taxes $458, title insurance $350, total credits $34,370, prorations of rents $250, and earnest money deposit of $1,000. Based upon this information, determine the balance due to the seller from the buyer.*

   a. $5,550.42
   b. $6,385.25
   c. $4,238.06
   d. $7,850.00

83. **A land developer wants to divide a 15-acre tract of land into lots that are each 50 feet x 120 feet. If the developer allowed 50,000 square feet for streets, how many lots can be developed in the subdivision?**

    a. 104
    b. 102
    c. 100
    d. 101

84. **What is the primary purpose of a deed?**

    a. Transfer of title
    b. Proof of ownership
    c. Recordation
    d. Legal evidence

85. **The Burkes, who own their house free of any encumbrance, are selling it to the Irwins for $145,000. The purchase price is to be paid by the Irwins, as follows: earnest money deposit of $3,000 and a cash payment of $42,000, with the Burkes taking back an amortized loan on the house for $100,000 at 12% interest for 15 years. This mortgage arrangement is best described as a:**

    a. Junior mortgage
    b. Partially amortized mortgage
    c. Wraparound mortgage
    d. Purchase money mortgage

86. **The first step in the appraisal process is:**

    a. Reconcile data
    b. Gather data
    c. Define the problem
    d. Inspect the property

87. **Which of the following would have first priority?**

    a. First mortgage
    b. IRS tax lien
    c. Mechanics lien
    d. Ad valorem taxes

88. **What type of ownership does a condominium owner hold?**

    a. Fee simple
    b. Estate in trust
    c. Proprietary lease
    d. Group ownership

89. **Earnest money is:**

    a. Determined by local custom
    b. Determined by the real estate broker or salesperson
    c. Fixed by law
    d. Not required for a valid purchase contract

90. **In a real estate transaction, the principal would best be described as:**

    a. The seller
    b. The buyer
    c. The person you represent
    d. All of the above

91. **Conventional loans:**

    a. Never have PMI
    b. Are insured by FHA
    c. Are guaranteed by VA
    d. Are not insured by the federal government

92. **Who would not need a real estate license?**

    a. An attorney selling real estate in an estate
    b. A salesperson working on a commission for a builder
    c. A property management company
    d. A friend selling a neighbor's lot for $1,000

93. **All of the following are essential to a valid contract, except:**

    a. Consideration
    b. Profit potential
    c. Offer and acceptance
    d. Legality of objective

94. **A buyer agrees to buy a house for $47,000, obtaining a 90% loan, and makes a deposit of $2,500. If attorney fees are $225, how much will the buyer need to bring to closing?**

    a. $2,425
    b. $4,700
    c. $42,525
    d. $44,725

95. **Wally got a second mortgage for $1,500 at 9% interest only for two years. What was the amount of principal due?**

    a. $1,230
    b. $1,365
    c. $1,500
    d. $1,770

96. *Section 36 of a township can be found where?*

a. NE corner of the township
b. NW corner of the township
c. SE corner of the township
d. SW corner of the township

97. *The responsibility for recording a deed lies with:*

a. Grantor
b. Grantee
c. County
d. State

98. *A latent defect is best described as:*

a. A defect that a prudent buyer can see
b. An old defect
c. A defect that is hidden from view
d. A breach of contract by the seller

99. *An offeror may withdraw the offer until:*

a. The closing date
b. The deed is recorded
c. The offer is signed
d. He or she is notified that the offer has been accepted

100. *The definition of depreciation is:*

a. A loss in value
b. Mortgage foreclosure
c. A loss from scarcity of a product
d. Negative amortization

Real Estate Exam #2

1. *In allegations of discriminatory practices under the Federal Fair Housing Act, the burden of proof is on the:*
   a. Court
   b. Defendant
   c. Complainant
   d. Department of Housing and Urban Development

2. *The Jones, with the consent of the previous owner, have had access to their pasture for more than 30 years through the previous owner's property. Thus,*
   a. The Jones can continue using the property through easement by implication
   b. The Jones have the potential right of ownership to this property because of the outright, notorious possession
   c. The Jones have the right to continue this use of the property through an easement by prescription
   d. The Jones own this property by adverse possession

3. *Which of the following charges is used to increase the lender's yield on a real estate loan?*
   a. Credit report
   b. Appraisal
   c. Title insurance
   d. Origination fee

4. *A mortgage that covers several parcels of land and contains a provision that allows for the sale of an individual parcel with clear title is called:*
   a. A direct reduction mortgage
   b. An amortized mortgage
   c. A blanket mortgage
   d. A declining balance mortgage

5. *A competitive market analysis is performed when:*
   a. Assessing property
   b. Pricing property
   c. Appraising property
   d. Condemning property

6. *The owner of a parcel of land sold it at a profit of 22%. The sales price was $17,500. What did the seller pay for the property?*
   a. $15,750.00
   b. $19,250.00
   c. $14,344.26
   d. $13,650.01

7. *How much cash will a buyer need at closing after depositing a $7,000 earnest money deposit with the seller's broker and acquiring a mortgage loan for 65 percent of the $48,500 sales price on a property being purchased?*
   a. $ 9,975
   b. $16,975
   c. $41,500
   d. $24,525

8. *A lot 100 feet wide and 175 feet deep was purchased at $250 per front foot. If a one-story building 75 feet by 40 feet was constructed on it at a cost of $17.20 per square foot, what was the combined cost of the land and the building?*
   a. $51,600
   b. $54,100
   c. $76,600
   d. $95,350

9. *An eight-year-old building is worth $119,000 after depreciating at a rate of 3% per year. What was its original value?*
   a. $122,680.41
   b. $156,578.95
   c. $119,357.00
   d. $147,560.00

10. *Which of the following best describes an installment contract or land contract?*
    a. A contract to buy land only
    b. A mortgage on land
    c. A means of conveying title immediately while a buyer pays for the property
    d. A method of selling real estate whereby the buyer pays for the property in regular installments while the seller retains title to the property

11. **Which of the following is not required of an agent with respect to the principal?**

a. Loyalty

b. To act in person

c. To account for the agent's own personal finances

d. To act in the principal's best interests

12. **Contracts made by a minor are:**

a. Void

b. Voidable by the minor

c. Voidable by all parties

d. Voidable by non-minor parties

13. **What is usury?**

a. Collecting more interest than that allowed by law

b. Building a structure that extends over someone else's land

c. Selling property for less than the asking price

d. Selling real estate without a license

14. **Robert bought a rectangular lot, 75 feet by 200 feet, that sold for $1.45 per square foot. The brokerage fee is 10%. How much is the fee?**

a. $ 150

b. $ 217

c. $2,175

d. $1,500

15. **Which is the superior lien?**

a. First mortgage

b. IRS tax lien

c. Mechanic's lien

d. Real estate taxes

16. **Ms. Fisher wants to net $17,500 from the sale of her property. A prospective buyer wants Ms. Fisher to pay a 2% service fee on a $15,000 loan. If she must pay a 6% brokerage fee and a 2% service fee. What is the minimum selling price?**

a. $18,936

b. $18,914

c. $19,000

d. $21,700

17. **Wayne's land has an easement to cross Fred's land to get to the lake. Wayne subdivides his land into two parcels and sells to Jane. Which statement is true?**

a. The easement no longer exists

b. Wayne's remaining land retains the easement, but Jane's does not

c. Both Wayne's remaining land and Jane's land have the easement rights

d. Land benefiting from an easement cannot be subdivided

18. **The law that requires that all transfers of ownership rights in real estate must be in writing is the:**

a. Statute of frauds

b. Statute of limitations

c. Parole evidence rule

d. Statute of liberties

19. **How much will the seller net from this sale based on the following: selling price $50,000; buyer to obtain a new FHA-insured loan for $48,000; buyer to pay 1 percent loan fee; seller to pay 3 discount points, 6% commission, $400 title insurance, plus $200 in other closing costs; seller to pay off existing loan of $24,250 which includes all principal and interest?**

a. $21,270

b. $20,710

c. $27,850

d. $20,770

20. **Common elements in a residential condominium usually include all the following, except:**

a. Stairways

b. Parking stalls assigned to particular apartments

c. Elevators

d. Roofs

21. **Which principle says that the highest value of a property is usually established by the cost of purchasing or constructing a building of equal utility and desirability?**

a. Principle of highest and best use

b. Principle of competition

c. Principle of supply and demand

d. Principle of substitution

22. **A building now twenty-one years old has a total economic life of forty years. If the original value of the building was $1,200,000, what is the value today?**

    a. $570,000
    b. $228,571
    c. $630,000
    d. $252,631

23. **Sandy, a licensed salesperson with Cobra Realty Co., had a listing that was sold by Sam, another salesperson with the same company. After the sale was consummated, but before closing, Sandy transferred to another real estate company. What should be done with Sandy's share of the commission?**

    a. It should be paid directly to Sandy by Cobra Realty Co.
    b. It should be paid to Sam
    c. It should be paid to Sandy's new broker to be passed on to Sandy
    d. It should be retained by Cobra Realty Co. and paid to no one

24. **The Fredericks want to buy an income property that grosses $300 per month. If the total annual expenses on this property are $1,200 and the Fredericks want a 12 percent return on their investment, how much should they offer for this property?**

    a. $36,000
    b. $24,000
    c. $28,800
    d. $20,000

25. **Which of the following statements is true?**

    a. All liens are encumbrances
    b. All encumbrances are liens
    c. Specific liens affect all property of the debtor located in the state
    d. Judgments are specific liens

26. **While walking in the basement, the real estate agent sees a leaky wall hidden behind some boxes. Who should disclose this defect?**

    a. The seller should, since this is an obvious patent defect
    b. The buyer should discover this latent defect
    c. It should be noted on the agency disclosure form
    d. The agent should immediately disclose the defect to the buyer

27. **If the closing date is November 10 and the seller has paid the real property taxes of $2,880 for the current tax year of January 1 through December 31, which of the following will be correct closing statement entry for taxes?**

    a. Seller's debit $2,477.59
    b. Seller's credit $402.41
    c. Buyer's credit $402.41
    d. Buyer's debit $2,477.59

28. **The buyer assumed a seller's 11%, $74,000 mortgage at closing on July 12. The seller had made the mortgage payment of $773.34, including principal and interest for July, on July 1 (using a 30-day month). What is the correct closing statement entry for interest?**

    a. Buyer's credit $406.98
    b. Seller's credit $271.32
    c. Buyer's debit $406.98
    d. Seller's debit $271.32

29. **A sales contract provided that the buyer was to pay $65,000 for a seller's property by giving a purchase money mortgage for $30,000 and the balance in cash at closing. The buyer made a good faith deposit of $6,500 when the offer was made. The seller's share of the real property taxes credited to the buyer was $850. The buyer's other closing costs totaled $900. What amount must the buyer pay at closing?**

    a. $35,050
    b. $27,700
    c. $27,650
    d. $28,550

30. **Simpson sells Bay Acres Farm to Baker, who does not record the deed. Simpson then makes a gift of Bay Acres to Freddie by way of a deed, which Freddie then records.**

   a. Because Freddie recorded his deed before Baker, Freddie has better title to Bay Acres than Baker

   b. Baker has better title than Freddie since Freddie is not a bona fide purchaser for value

   c. Baker has superior title to Freddie since a deed was given to Baker first

   d. A recorded deed takes priority over all others, regardless of how the grantee acquires title

31. **An owner requests a broker to list a property for sale at $70,000. Upon inspection, the broker believes the property is worth $80,000. The broker should:**

   a. Get a listing for the property at $70,000

   b. Buy the property for $70,000

   c. Inform the seller that the property is worth $80,000

   d. Tell the owner to list the property at $75,000, so there's room to bargain

32. **Abandoned private property redeemed by local government is an example of:**

   a. Police power

   b. Eminent domain

   c. Taxation

   d. Escheat

33. **A broker is holding an earnest money deposit, equal to the amount of the commission. The seller, at the closing, not only refuses to pay the broker a commission but also demands the broker pay the seller the entire deposit, to which the buyer agrees. The broker should:**

   a. Refuse to permit the closing of the deal

   b. Retain the earnest money as commission

   c. File a complaint with the state Real Estate Division

   d. Pay the earnest money to the seller and then sue for the commission

34. **If fire destroys a home after the contract of sale is signed by both parties, but prior to closing, all of the following are true, except:**

   a. The party in possession generally bears the risk of loss

   b. The seller bears all risk of loss if in possession and holding legal title at the time of the loss

   c. The buyer assumes responsibility upon signing the sales contract

   d. Responsibility generally passes to the buyer upon closing

35. **Russell Minor, 16-years-old and unmarried, employs Snappy Realty under an exclusive right-to-sell listing to sell an apartment building Russell inherited from his father. Snappy Realty finds Ready Buyer who executes a sales contract on the complete listing terms, which the seller accepts. Which of the following statements is true?**

   a. Russell can void the contract with Ready Buyer

   b. Russell is liable to Snappy Realty for the full commission

   c. The contract is voidable by the buyer

   d. The contract is binding on both parties

36. **An apartment rents only to "singles." Refusal to rent to which of the following would result in a violation of the Federal Fair Housing Act?**

   a. Families

   b. Elderly persons

   c. Military officers

   d. None of the above

37. **A lending institution will make a 30-year 9½% loan for 70 percent of the first $50,000 and 40% for the next $45,000 of the appraised value. If a house is appraised at $95,000, what will be the first month's interest charge?**

   a. $419.58

   b. $752.08

   c. $526.46

   d. $300.83

38. *As commission for negotiating the sale of a $900,000 hotel, a broker received title to a piece of land valued at $30,000. The same day the hotel escrow closed, the broker sold the land for $40,000. Which is true about the broker's action in selling the land?*

a. This is proper as long as the broker received title before reselling the land

b. Such action violates the licensing law if the broker does not give written notice to the hotel client of the sale

c. It is illegal to receive land as a commission

d. Such action violates the licensing law because of the secret profit

39. *According to the law of agency as it relates to a broker:*

a. Brokers must always charge commission and put the amount on a listing form

b. A broker may sue and collect a commission even though the broker had a suspended license when the commission was earned

c. The commission must always be based on the listed price

d. The principal and the client are the same person

40. *Sammy Seller and Betty Buyer will close on Seller's house July 9, 2003. Property taxes for 2002 were paid by Seller based on the property assessed at $16,500, combined tax rate of $3.25 per $100 of assessed value. If taxes were last paid for the 2nd half of 2002, what amount of prorated taxes is due to the buyer?*

a. $281.53

b. $257.11

c. $279.14

d. $672.12

41. *If a mortgagor defaults on the note:*

a. The mortgagor is given a 6-month grace period to bring the account current

b. The mortgage becomes due and payable

c. The mortgagee may begin a non-judicial foreclosure proceeding right away

d. All of the above

42. *To the owner of land it runs across, an easement is:*

a. An appurtenance

b. An encumbrance

c. A common interest

d. An attachment

43. *Discount points are charged by the lender:*

a. To lower the closing costs

b. To help a mortgagor with a down payment

c. To lower the interest rate

d. All of the above

44. *What is the fullest estate a property owner can have?*

a. Fee simple divisible

b. Full unity of possession

c. Tenancy for years

d. Fee simple absolute

45. *The Fair Housing Act prohibits:*

a. Discrimination in housing because of race

b. Discrimination in residential renting

c. Discrimination in housing because of religion

d. All of the above

46. *A warranty deed guarantees against all of the following, except:*

a. The grantor's heirs

b. Easements of record

c. Mortgages

d. Judgment liens

47. *A valid contract requires only:*

a. Consideration

b. Recordation

c. Offer, acceptance, and consideration

d. To be placed in writing and signed

48. *The person who hires another to represent him or her is known as:*

a. A customer

b. A client

c. A broker

d. An agent

49. **A listing broker receives an offer that fully matches the listing terms. Before presenting the offer, the broker receives two more offers, one for less than the listing price, but for cash, and one for more than the listing price, but the seller is to take back a mortgage. What is the best approach for the listing broker?**

   a. Present the offer for the highest price

   b. Present all offers at the same time

   c. Present the cash offer first

   d. Present the offers in the order received, one at a time

50. **The lender in a mortgage relationship is the:**

   a. Mortgagee

   b. Mortgagor

   c. Trustee

   d. Beneficiary

51. **A note, as opposed to a mortgage, is a:**

   a. Lien

   b. Personal obligation

   c. Second mortgage

   d. Judgment

52. **If a lessor dies after all parties have signed a lease, the lease is:**

   a. Cancelled

   b. Renegotiated

   c. Unchanged

   d. Rescinded

53. **The value of property can be lowered by:**

   a. A changing neighborhood

   b. Economic obsolescence

   c. Zoning laws

   d. All of the above

54. **Essential elements for a deed include:**

   a. Signatures of grantor and grantee

   b. Words of conveyance

   c. Recording

   d. All of the above

55. **When does a deed convey title to property?**

   a. When it is signed

   b. When it is recorded

   c. When it is accepted

   d. When it is mortgaged

56. **An agency relationship is created between a principal and a real estate broker by a:**

   a. Sales agreement

   b. Listing contract

   c. Purchase offer

   d. All of the above

57. **Of the following signed documents, which is not covered by the Statute of Frauds?**

   a. Purchase contract

   b. Listing agreement

   c. Option on land

   d. Five-year commercial lease

58. **Title insurance protects policyholders from all of the following defects, except:**

   a. A forged deed

   b. Mistakes in the public record

   c. An unrecorded lien, which the buyer knew about

   d. Improper deeds

59. **A mortgage is acknowledged by:**

   a. Notary

   b. Mortgagors

   c. Mortgagee

   d. Closing officer

60. **If appraising a single-family home, which appraisal method would get the most weight?**

   a. Sales comparison approach

   b. Competitive market analysis (CMA)

   c. Income approach

   d. Cost approach

61. **A contract is entered into on fraudulent terms introduced by the seller. When the buyer learns of this, the contract would be:**
    a. Valid
    b. Void
    c. Voidable by the buyer
    d. Voidable by the seller

62. **All of the following show evidence of marketable title, except:**
    a. Abstract of title
    b. Certificate of title
    c. Title insurance
    d. Location survey

63. **Which of the following are covered under RESPA?**
    a. Prohibits kickbacks
    b. Requires use of HUD-1 settlement statement
    c. Limits escrow reserves a lender can require
    d. All of the above

64. **Which of the following are not security instruments for real estate?**
    a. Promissory notes
    b. Mortgages
    c. Trust deeds
    d. Land contracts

65. **Pat wants to buy an investment property and share ownership with two adult children. Pat will keep 2/3 ownership and the children will share 1/3 ownership. How will they take title?**
    a. Tenants by the entireties
    b. Joint tenants with right of survivorship
    c. Tenants in common
    d. Tenants with a survivorship deed

66. **Which of the following is the largest, privately owned secondary market player?**
    a. FHLMC
    b. FDIC
    c. FNMA
    d. GNMA

67. **A fully amortized loan means that the loan will be paid off:**
    a. In equal monthly installments over 30 years
    b. In equal monthly installments with a balloon payment
    c. In equal monthly installments of interest-only payments
    d. In equal monthly installments that pay off the entire balance during the loan term

68. **When a counteroffer is made, what happens to the original offer?**
    a. It is held in a secondary position
    b. It is deemed rejected
    c. It can be used as a fall back position if the counteroffer is rejected
    d. It is considered a novation

69. **Equitable title is:**
    a. An interest in real property created by the execution of a valid sales contract
    b. Actual lawful ownership of real property
    c. Evidence of title
    d. An instrument that conveys ownership of real property

70. **Alice and Conrad bought a house and got a general warranty deed. Later, they learn that the previous owner's wife didn't release dower. What's the easiest way to take care of this?**
    a. Have the owner and his wife execute another general warranty deed
    b. Have the owner execute a quitclaim deed
    c. Have the owner's wife execute a quitclaim deed
    d. Have the owner and his wife issue a wild deed

71. **A licensed real estate broker:**
    a. Can disclose any true information received from the principal
    b. Becomes an agent of the vendor only when a buyer is found
    c. Becomes an agent of the vendee on obtaining a valid listing
    d. Must disclose all material facts to the principal

72. **At what point does a broker deposit funds to the trust account?**

    a. They must go immediately into the trust account

    b. According to the terms of the purchase contract

    c. It's okay to hold them until the agreement is signed

    d. 10 days

73. **An agent can advertise a property for sale under the agent's own name if:**

    a. The agent is a member of the local real estate board

    b. The agent personally listed the property

    c. The agent personally paid for the ad

    d. The official name of the agent's broker is also in the ad

74. **A licensed salesperson is authorized by law in most states to:**

    a. Sign a purchase and sale agreement on behalf of the principal

    b. Act only under the supervision of a real estate broker

    c. Advertise property under the salesperson's own name

    d. Collect a commission directly from a principal

75. **To be entitled to a commission, the listing broker must:**

    a. Be licensed when the commission is earned

    b. Be a member of a multiple listing service

    c. Have a contract with the seller broker

    d. Have a seller statement signed

76. **A property manager is usually responsible for:**

    a. Renting space to tenants

    b. Preparing a budget

    c. Developing a management plan

    d. All of the above

77. **The closing statement shows debits and credits accorded to each party in the transaction. A debit is a/an:**

    a. Refund

    b. Expense

    c. Post-closing adjustment

    d. Proration

78. **Three children wish to purchase their parents' home. They wish to acquire the title so that the last child to die will own the property 100%. Which of the following is the best way for them to take title?**

    a. Tenancy in the entireties

    b. Tenancy per child

    c. Joint tenancy

    d. Tenancy in common

79. **A warranty (covenant) in a deed protects against which of the following?**

    a. Property taxes

    b. City health laws

    c. Recorded restrictive uses of the property

    d. Unrecorded mechanic's lien that the seller knew about

80. **Federally related first mortgages, according to RESPA (Real Estate Settlement Procedures Act) include:**

    a. Commercial property and four-family dwellings

    b. One-family dwellings and four-family dwellings

    c. One-family dwellings

    d. One-family dwellings, four-family dwellings, and commercial property

81. **A land contract:**

    a. Is a contract on raw land

    b. Conveys title to the vendor from the vendee

    c. Is a way for the vendor to help the vendee finance the property

    d. Is none of the above

82. **What is the purpose of a buydown?**

    a. To help a buyer qualify for a home more easily

    b. To help the seller make a home more attractive to purchase

    c. To help a buyer get into a bigger home

    d. All of the above

83. **Under Truth in Lending, the borrower has:**

    a. 1 year to rescind

    b. 30 days to rescind

    c. 3 business days to change his or her mind

    d. Cannot change his or her mind

84. **The type of mortgage that permits a borrower to borrow an additional sum in the future is called a/an:**
   a. Blanket loan
   b. Open end loan
   c. Swing loan
   d. Package mortgage

85. **An appraiser who was estimating the value of a four-story government building determined that each floor measured 90 feet by 80 feet with a replacement cost of $60 per square foot. The appraiser also observed that the building had depreciated 25%, as the result of physical and functional obsolescence. Other site improvements were estimated to have depreciated 20%, from a new value of $160,000. The appraiser also estimated the land associated with the building to be worth $362,000. What is the correct value estimate of the property value by the cost approach?**
   a. $ 814,000
   b. $1,786,000
   c. $1,818,000
   d. $ 846,000

86. **The most common method of estimating property value for fire insurance purposes is:**
   a. Market comparison
   b. Gross income
   c. Replacement cost
   d. Anticipated use

87. **The Aspen Apartment Complex, valued at $550,000, has a gross rent multiplier of 6.5 and has operating expenses at 35%. What would be the net operating income?**
   a. $ 36,450
   b. $ 85,793
   c. $ 55,000
   d. $127,534

88. **Which one of the following deeds contains the most covenants?**
   a. General warranty
   b. Quitclaim
   c. Grant
   d. Bargain and sale

89. **Smith sells her property to Baker and gives Baker a special warranty deed. Which is true?**
   a. Smith is making more warranties than would be found in a warranty deed
   b. Smith's property is registered under the Torrens system
   c. Smith is warranting that there have never been any liens against the property that are now unpaid
   d. Smith's warranties are limited to the time when she owned the property

90. **Which of the following is a lien on real estate?**
   a. Easement
   b. Mortgage
   c. License
   d. Encroachment

91. **Which of the following is true with respect to lien priority?**
   a. A mechanic's lien is always first in priority
   b. The date of the lien determines priority
   c. The date the lien is recorded establishes priority (except mechanic's liens)
   d. The size of the lien determines priority

92. **A real estate tax lien takes priority over which of the following?**
   a. An encroachment
   b. An easement
   c. A deed restriction
   d. A mortgage

93. **Rescission of a contract is best defined as which of the following?**
   a. Ratification of a contract by all parties
   b. The voiding of a contract
   c. A revision in the terms of a contract
   d. A transfer of responsibility from one of a contract's parties to a third party

94. **A purchase contract exists between buyer and seller. Buyer wishes to substitute another qualified buyer with all other terms remaining the same. This is:**
   a. A novation
   b. A unilateral contract
   c. An assignment
   d. A voidable contract

95. **What's the legal procedure (action) brought by a buyer to enforce terms of a contract?**

   a. An injunction
   b. Specific performance
   c. Lis pendens
   d. An attachment

96. **Busey enters into a contract to purchase Turner's house for $110,000. Busey cannot get bank financing, and negotiates a land contract agreement with Turner. Upon signing the contract for deed, Busey's interest in the property is that of:**

   a. Legal title
   b. Equitable title
   c. Mortgagor
   d. Mortgagee

97. **Consideration in a legally binding contract could be:**

   a. Money
   b. A promise
   c. A refrigerator
   d. Any of the above

98. **A deed that conveys title to a mortgagee from a mortgagor and avoids the necessity of legal action to recover the lender's collateral is known as a deed:**

   a. Of surrender
   b. In lieu of foreclosure
   c. Of release
   d. Of reconveyance

99. **Gray buys Blue's home with the help of a loan from a bank. The bank insists Gray obtain an extended coverage title insurance policy. The policy:**

   a. Protects Gray from all adverse claims
   b. Indemnifies against some, but not all, adverse claims
   c. Insures Blue against any defects caused while Blue owned the property
   d. Insures Blue, Gray, and the bank against any abnormal claims

100. **How many cubic feet are in a storage area 15 yards wide, 15 feet deep, and 12 feet high?**

   a. 2700 cubic feet
   b. 225 cubic feet
   c. 8100 cubic feet
   d. 675 cubic feet

REAL ESTATE EXAM #1: ANSWERS

1. . . . . . b	51. . . . . .b	1. c	51. . . . . .b
2. c	52. . . . . .a	2. . . . . . a	52. c
3. . . . . . b	53. . . . .d	3. . . . . . d	53. . . . .d
4. . . . . . b	54. . . . .b	4. c	54. . . . .b
5. . . . . b	55. . . . .d	5. . . . . . b	55. c
6. c	56. . . . .a	6. c	56. . . . .b
7. . . . . a	57. . . . .b	7. . . . . . a	57. . . . .b
8. c	58. c	8. c	58. c
9. . . . . a	59. . . . .b	9. . . . . b	59. . . . .b
10. . . . . d	60. . . . .a	10. . . . . d	60. . . . . .a
11. . . . . . b	61. . . . .b	11. c	61. c
12. . . . . a	62. . . . .a	12. . . . . a	62. . . . .d
13. . . . . d	63. . . . .d	13. . . . . a	63. . . . .d
14. . . . . b	64. . . . .d	14. c	64. . . . . a
15. c	65. c	15. . . . . d	65. c
16. . . . . a	66. . . . .d	16. . . . . a	66. c
17. c	67. . . . .d	17. c	67. . . . .d
18. . . . . d	68. . . . .a	18. . . . . a	68. . . . .b
19. . . . . d	69. . . . .a	19. . . . . b	69. . . . .a
20. . . . . a	70. c	20. . . . . b	70. c
21. . . . . a	71. . . . .b	21. . . . . d	71. . . . .d
22. . . . . b	72. . . . .d	22. . . . . a	72. . . . .b
23. . . . . b	73. . . . .b	23. . . . . a	73. . . . .d
24. . . . . d	74. c	24. . . . . d	74. . . . .b
25. c	75. . . . . b	25. . . . . a	75. . . . .a
26. c	76. . . . . d	26. . . . . d	76. . . . .d
27. . . . . b	77. . . . . b	27. . . . . b	77. . . . .b
28. . . . . b	78. c	28. c	78. c
29. . . . . a	79. c	29. . . . . d	79. . . . .d
30. . . . . b	80. . . . . d	30. . . . . b	80. . . . .b
31. . . . . d	81. . . . . b	31. . . . c	81. c
32. . . . . d	82. c	32. . . . d	82. . . . .d
33. . . . . b	83. c	33. . . . d	83. c
34. c	84. . . . .a	34. . . . c	84. . . . .b
35. . . . . d	85. . . . . d	35. . . . . a	85. . . . .b
36. . . . . b	86. c	36. . . . . a	86. c
37. . . . . a	87. . . . . d	37. . . . a	87. c
38. . . . . a	88. . . . .a	38. . . . d	88. . . . .a
39. . . . . a	89. . . . . d	39. . . . d	89. . . . .d
40. . . . . a	90. c	40. . . . c	90. . . . .b
41. . . . . b	91. . . . .d	41. . . . b	91. c
42. . . . . b	92. . . . . .a	42. . . . b	92. . . . . .d
43. . . . . d	93. . . . .b	43. c	93. . . . .b
44. . . . . a	94. . . . .a	44. . . . d	94. c
45. c	95. c	45. . . . d	95. . . . .b
46. . . . . b	96. c	46. . . . b	96. . . . .b
47. . . . . b	97. . . . . b	47. . . . c	97. . . . .d
48. c	98. c	48. . . . b	98. . . . .b
49. . . . . d	99. . . . .d	49. . . . b	99. . . . .b
50. . . . . d	100. . . .a	50. . . . a	100. . . .c

REAL ESTATE EXAM #2: ANSWERS